Winds of Change

The Life and Legacy of Calvin W. Ruck

Lindsay R. Ruck

Pottersfield Press, Lawrencetown Beach, Nova Scotia, Canada

Copyright © Lindsay Ruck 2014

All rights reserved. No part of this publication may be reproduced or used or stored in any form or by any means – graphic, electronic or mechanical, including photocopying – or by any information storage or retrieval system without the prior written permission of the publisher. Any requests for photocopying, recording, taping or information storage and retrieval systems shall be directed in writing to the publisher. This also applies to classroom use.

Library and Archives Canada Cataloguing in Publication

Ruck, Lindsay R., author
    Winds of change : the life and legacy of Calvin W. Ruck / Lindsay R. Ruck.
ISBN 978-1-897426-57-9 (pbk.)
1. Ruck, Calvin W. (Calvin Woodrow), 1925-2004. 2. Legislators--Nova Scotia--Biography.
3. Social workers--Nova Scotia--Biography. 4. Historians-- Nova Scotia--Biography. I. Title.
FC2349.S93Z49 2014   971.6'9504092   C2013-907927-0

Cover design by Gail LeBlanc

We acknowledge the financial support of the Government of Canada through the Canada Book Fund for our publishing activities. We acknowledge the support of the Canada Council for the Arts, which last year invested $157 million to bring the arts to Canadians throughout the country. Nous remercions le Conseil des arts du Canada de son soutien. L'an dernier, le Conseil a investi 157 millions de dollars pour mettre de l'art dans la vie des Canadiennes et des Canadiens de tout le pays. Pottersfield Press recognizes the support of the Province of Nova Scotia through Film and Creative Industries Nova Scotia. We are pleased to work in partnership with the agency to develop and promote our creative industries for the benefit of all Nova Scotians.

Pottersfield Press
83 Leslie Road
East Lawrencetown, Nova Scotia, Canada, B2Z 1P8
Website: www.PottersfieldPress.com
To order, phone 1-800-NIMBUS9 (1-800-646-2879) www.nimbus.ns.ca

*To my grandmother, Joyce Alice Mae Ruck
– the woman beside the man*

"I recall going into a barbershop run by the president of the barber's union in Dartmouth, Nova Scotia. I do not know if other honourable senators have ever sat in the chair of an angry barber. It is a frightening thing. He was very angry because he knew I was within my rights to receive service from him. I told that barber that to refuse to serve me was to break the law. The human rights people visited him and straightened him out. We have come a long way, indeed. We have run into stumbling blocks, but the winds of change have blown."

– Calvin W. Ruck

Contents

From The Author	7
1: From Small Beginnings	9
2: No Vacancy	17
3: Rising Above	35
4: Pushing Past The City Lines	43
5: A House Is Not A Home	54
6: We Serve	65
7: Canada's Best Kept Military Secret	75
8: Triumph And Tragedy	87
9: Senator Ruck	94
10: No Place Like Home	106
11: Leaving A Legacy	115
Conclusion	125

Calvin Ruck's official Senate photo.

From The Author

It is probably a person's greatest and proudest accomplishment to write an autobiography, and had my grandfather not become legally blind and been diagnosed with Alzheimer's disease, perhaps this would have been his next project (although he found more pleasure telling others' stories than his own). As his mind continued to deteriorate, I realized this was not going to happen. But I knew whether it was from his pen or mine, the story had to be told.

In the early stages, when this project was still just an idea, I quickly discovered I had entire communities behind me. And although my name is on the cover, this is not my book. This story is told by the many (but unfortunately not all) who knew and loved my grandfather as a colleague, brother, and friend. As I listened to anecdote upon anecdote from those who were changed by one man's actions and encouraging words, I suddenly became overwhelmed with emotion and self-doubt. I realized exactly what I had taken on and the question, "How do you do a man justice who is considered a Canadian hero?" crept into my mind.

In a family like mine, however, you don't have much time for negative thinking. My sister, Jacqueline, and I are constantly reminded by our father, Doug, and mother, Valerie, that we can accomplish anything, big or small. While my grandfather was great, he was also fearless, and that is in my blood. His story is a testament that anyone can do anything and I reminded myself of that message throughout this labour of love.

My relationship with my grandfather was a simple one. I did not attend the meetings where he rallied for change; I was not by his side when the hate mail and threats entered his home. I was there to see his accomplishments. I looked on as he was praised for his many years of community activism and social justice. I am so grateful to everyone who provided me with the bigger picture.

Ruck is not just a last name. Because of my grandfather, Ruck is spoken with admiration, written about in the highest regard and will forever be remembered as a great legacy. If I am honest, I will never truly believe I did my grandfather's incredible life story justice – but I was determined to come as close as I possibly could.

I hope I made you proud, Granddad.

1: From Small Beginnings

In the early 1900s, Sydney, Nova Scotia – "the Steel City," on Cape Breton's east coast – became the destination for a sizeable number of Caribbean immigrants. Known as "the later arrivals" because they followed earlier Black settlers to Nova Scotia, such as the Black Loyalists of the 1770s and the Black Refugees of the War of 1812, they came to find work in the steel mills and coal mines in Sydney and the towns of Glace Bay and New Waterford.

Calvin Ruck's parents, George and Ida (nee Inniss) Ruck were Bajan immigrants. Calvin, born September 4, 1925, along with his three brothers, Lionel, Winston and Arthur, and foster brother, Vernol Braithwaite, grew up in Whitney Pier, an area on the northern boundary of Sydney. After the children's mother died when Calvin was two, Calvin's father was left to care for five boys. He found work wherever he could to support his young family. Running a strict household, George Ruck made sure the boys always did what they were told and when visitors arrived at the house, the boys were sent outside. Calvin and his brothers were never allowed to wander too far from home, and if one child ever became bold enough to travel more than a street or two over, then each boy was punished for the misdemeanour.

When Calvin's father passed away, the boys were taken under the care of Aunt V (Viola), who lived on Tupper Street in the Pier. Aunt V was George's sister. "It seemed as if parents were dying at a young age

Calvin's parents, George Ruck and Ida Inniss Ruck.

in Sydney during those days and the Ruck boys were quite young when both their parents passed away," says Roland (Rollie) Callendar. Rollie was raised by his mother, but after her passing, he joined the Ruck boys on Tupper Street. "Aunt V was actually my grandmother (my mother's mother), but I always called her Aunt V like everyone else," explains Rollie. "We were very poor, but my memories of those times are good. This was the only family I knew and when I was young I used to call Winston, Calvin and Lionel my uncles, even though they always treated me as if I was their younger brother."

Described as a spiritual woman who always carried a Bible with her, Aunt V had a heart for children and raised them as though they were her own. "Aunt V was a very kind and mild-mannered person, and I never heard her say a bad thing about anyone," recalls Rollie. "Neither did I ever

A family portrait. Back row, left to right, are Vernol Braithwaite and Winston. Front row, left to right, are Calvin, Lionel, Arthur, and George.

hear anyone say a bad word about her. She was well respected and a real lady. I would say she went out of her way to be kind to everyone and just had so much love for all of us. She truly loved the Ruck boys and even after they had left, she would tell me to pray for them every night and I always did." Every Sunday, the family attended church, but as soon as the service was over they would return home and change immediately as what they wore to church was only for Sundays and special occasions.

Aunt V instilled in them a sense of right and wrong, and just as Calvin's father had done, made sure they were always respectful and well-mannered – something each of them remembered for the rest of their lives.

"I have no doubt that she had a major influence on all of us," says Rollie. "I saw her sense of right and good reflected in the way the brothers handled themselves. Calvin was always a very decent and caring person even when young. I feel he saw the way Aunt V conducted herself and Calvin was influenced by her. Aunt V made sure we were always respectful to adults and we were never allowed to call anyone older than us by their first name. It had to be Mr. or Mrs. So and So. If the person was a close friend of the family, we were allowed to call them aunt or uncle."

The boys' spare time was mostly spent playing sports, favouring both hockey and baseball. When Calvin and Winston were still quite young they decided to build an outdoor ice rink at the end of Tupper Street. The makeshift rink was an inexpensive way to have fun. "They used to clear an area and put boards around for the sides," explains Rollie. "They would clear and flood the ice and the kids in the neighbourhood would skate and play hockey. Calvin was a really good hockey player."

When they weren't playing hockey, they would listen to games on the radio. "There was no TV back then," says Rollie. "We would listen to the games and the brothers would teach me the names of the players. Calvin would try to get me to learn different things by repeating things to me. Even though I was younger than them, they always included me in what they were doing."

Whether on the ice or in school, the Ruck boys were constantly competing, which motivated them to work harder and excel in everything they did. "They always wanted to see who could do the best," explains

Calvin as a young man.

Rollie. "There was something in them that made them work very hard to better themselves and others around them. They were exceptional that way and we saw it in Calvin throughout his entire life."

Along with the Ruck boys, Rollie, and Vernol, Aunt V also took in a young girl who had lost her parents. "She was raised with us as if she was our sister," says Rollie. "I don't know how Aunt V managed to care for all of us. I know that people would come to the house and she would braid their hair, but I do not know if she was paid to do it."

The blended family lived in a long, rundown building that housed several families. Race was not really an issue in the neighbourhood, as Rollie recalls everyone had one thing in common – poverty. "The neighbourhood had a real mixture of people. There were Italians, Ukrainians, Greeks, Blacks and Jews. We all got along as we were all poor together."

Whether the funds were there or not, Aunt V somehow managed to support her children. "There were times she would ask me to go to the store and tell me she had no money but would give me a note to give to the store owner and he would give me rice to take home," recalls Rollie. "I guess she had some kind of credit arrangement with him."

Little money meant the young children really didn't have many toys to play with, which is why a random gesture from Calvin has never been forgotten by his "little brother." "I remember that one time Calvin bought me a big red toy truck," recalls Rollie. "I don't recall that it was a special occasion or anything; he just got it for me. I never forgot about him doing that for me and I even mentioned it to him many years later. He was surprised that I remembered him giving me the truck, but it really meant a lot to me."

Despite Aunt V providing a roof over their heads, Calvin knew he had to also start contributing and helping out however he could. In grade ten, Calvin dropped out of high school. In 1942 he began working full-time as a labourer at the Dominion Steel and Coal Mill. The pay was minimal and the work was rugged, but at that time, it was the only option for a Black man to make a living.

In 1945, Calvin moved to Halifax to join the ranks of the Canadian National Railway as a sleeping car porter. Life as a porter meant extensive travelling, long hours and servitude to the paying passengers. In *A Dignity Denied: The Black Porter on Canadian National Railways*, Jim Simmons describes the position of a sleeping car porter as "the highest status in the Black community and the lowest rank on the train. They were trapped into dual roles of charming hosts and menial, obedient servant." Porters were there to be at your every beck and call and there was no such thing as too onerous a task. Simmons goes on to say, "If passengers complained, the company would call you in and 'dress you down.' Many supervisors were unfair and at times docked your pay. They would fire people frequently."

An incident that illustrates one of the hardships of such employment occurred about 1952, when Calvin had been a sleeping car porter for about seven years. While Calvin was making beds, a passenger approached him requesting that he tend to *his* room and make *his* bed. Calvin politely addressed the man, assuring him that he would head to his

Calvin worked for CNR as a sleeping car porter from 1945 to 1958.

room once he was finished with the task at hand. Not willing to wait, the man stated he wanted the bed made immediately and he grabbed Calvin and pushed him. Calvin's reflexes got the best of him and he returned the shove. Enraged and most likely embarrassed by a porter showing some authority, the man reported Calvin immediately. Upon returning home, Calvin let his wife know that he may have just lost his job. A trial followed that gave Calvin a chance to explain his side of the story. Miraculously, Calvin was not let go and continued to work on the railway.

The hectic life of a porter was never-ending, allowing perhaps four hours of sleep on a good day. "The job included more than helping passengers with baggage or preparing their sleeping berths," continues Simmons. "If a passenger wanted to eat in his berth, the porter walked to the dining car for food. He babysat children, shined shoes, and ironed suits. He tended to the sick and still had to find time to keep the car clean." Sleeping car porters came face to face with racism and discrimination on a daily basis. Although Calvin and his peers knew how they were being treated wasn't right, many were too afraid to speak up as it could mean losing one of the few jobs Blacks were able to get at that time.

Despite being grateful to have found employment, Calvin was extremely unhappy and knew he couldn't do this for the rest of his life. While work may have been strenuous, Calvin was about to find the silver lining of his move to the province's capital of Halifax. Her name was Joyce Alice Mae Williams.

A young Calvin in Quebec City.

2: No Vacancy

At a small lunch counter in Halifax in 1946, sixteen-year-old Joyce Williams sat with her friend reading a magazine. Unbeknownst to Joyce, she was about to meet the man who would change her life forever.

When Calvin wasn't on the road, the twenty-year-old enjoyed playing sports and spending time with friends. On this particular day off, Calvin and his friend were walking down Cunard Street. They happened to look in and saw two young girls they had never seen before. Intrigued, and like any bold young men, they walked in and sat down right next to the young women and tried to get their attention. Calvin began reading aloud the cover of Joyce's magazine. Unimpressed by this attempt for attention, Joyce abruptly shut the magazine and refused to make eye contact with this boy who seemed so fascinated by her. Not that long after, Joyce and her companion left, hoping that would be the end of the awkward situation. Calvin, on the other hand, was determined to find out more about this pretty young woman. The boys quickly exited the restaurant and followed the girls. With a little charm and a lot of luck, Calvin managed to get Joyce's name, phone number and even the privilege of walking her home that day. A few days later, Calvin called the Williams' residence and Joyce accepted an offer to go to the theatre. And so began a fifty-six-year romance.

Calvin and Joyce, Christmas 1950.

Joyce recounts Calvin's courtship as respectable and chivalrous. He was polite, kind, and as Joyce recalls, he "wasn't brazen. I can remember when we were walking one day and I felt his hand touch my lower back. I moved it right away and said that a man does not touch a lady's backside." Slightly embarrassed, Calvin quickly apologized numerous times, and at that moment, he knew that this girl whom he had met at the lunch counter was not like other girls. She was special.

"When he asked me to be his girlfriend, he said, 'You know you can't go out with other guys?'" Joyce recollects with a smile. But Joyce had no intention of seeing anyone else and at sixteen, she fell in love for the first and last time.

Two years later, with engagement ring in hand, Calvin asked Joyce to marry him, and this time, she didn't hesitate to respond, as she knew she had found the love of her life. Her father, however, was not as taken with this twenty-two-year-old sleeping car porter. Calvin's parents were both from Barbados and Emmanuel Williams wanted nothing to do with those of West Indian descent. Joyce tried to explain to her father that Calvin was born in Canada and was a Canadian citizen, but this did not matter and Joyce was left looking for someone else to give her away at her wedding. Having never shied away from a challenge, Calvin was determined to change this man's mind and to be accepted by his future father-in-law. Exhausting all words, one day Calvin offered Mr. Williams a cigarette. It may not have been your typical olive branch, but it was all that was needed to bring the two together. From that time on, Calvin was accepted as a worthy husband.

The Ruck-Williams wedding took place at Cornwallis Street Baptist Church in Halifax on August 18, 1948. Although Joyce's father was present on the day, her uncle, John Pannill, gave the bride away. Emmanuel, who worked odd jobs his whole life, including as a night watchman at a grain elevator, said he could not afford a suit for the occasion and was not comfortable walking his daughter down the aisle if he wasn't "properly" dressed. "I think that was just an excuse, though," says Joyce, adding that her father also stated she was much too young to be married. At eighteen, Joyce, who still wears her wedding ring to this day, says she was never nervous or had second thoughts when it came to marriage. She laughs and thinks, "Maybe it was because I just didn't know any better, or maybe it was just because I was marrying Calvin."

"They both had very distinct roles and they both fulfilled those roles to the best of their ability," says Calvin's granddaughter, Jacqueline Ruck, who describes the marriage as the "perfect partnership. He needed someone who was going to be able to take care of his children when he wasn't there and he needed someone who was able to have meals ready when he wasn't there. He respected Nanny for that role. I think they both just had a mutual understanding of what they had to do together and it was a good partnership."

It's been said that behind every good man is a good woman. In Calvin's case, it was always right beside. "They were a real team," says his colleague Joan Gilroy. "If it hadn't been for her, he wouldn't have been able to do a lot of what he did." Joyce's role in the home was just as important as Calvin's outside of the home. The pair discussed and made all decisions together, and Joyce says she always felt like his equal.

The newlyweds lived in the north end of Halifax, in a predominantly Black neighbourhood that mainly consisted of tenement homes, boarding rooms and apartments. About a year and a half after they had been married, the couple decided to start a family. In December 1949, when Joyce was eight months pregnant with their first child, they went to the Halifax Infirmary to request a semi-private room for the birth. Two nuns greeted them at the desk and blatantly said they did not have any semi-private rooms in their Infirmary and the couple would have to look elsewhere. With this news, Joyce and Calvin began to exit the hospital. Upon leaving, the secretary, who first greeted them at the front entrance, inquired if they were successful in booking the room. The couple relayed to her what the nuns had said to them and the secretary was surprised by the news, as she was fully aware that there were in fact semi-private rooms in the Infirmary. It was then clear to the couple that not everyone in the establishment wanted whites and Blacks sharing rooms, so they decided that Joyce would deliver at Grace Maternity, where there were plenty of semi-private rooms that catered to both Black and white women.

After the birth of their first son, Douglas, on January 12, 1950, Calvin returned to his job as a porter and spent weeks at a time on the road. During his absenses, he and Joyce would pen letters to one another:

May 2, 1951
Darling Joyce,

I received your welcome letter this morning and I was more than glad to hear from you. I am feeling well and I trust and hope that both you and little Dougie are well also and getting along well. I am now at the porter's quarters in Moncton and I have just finished supper.

I pray that some time in the not too distant future if everything goes good we may be fortunate enough to have a place to call our own.

Joyce I was very lonely last night in Rivière Du Loup before train time, but I just shrugged it off because I have a good while to go before I get to see you again. Little Dougie was so sweet the day I left. After I kissed you he was smacking his lips for me to kiss him. He is such a darling little boy, isn't he?

I will lay down and rest awhile before I prepare for work so I must bring this letter to a close hoping to hear from you soon. So until I see you keep remembering that I love you with all my heart.

Your loving husband,
Calvin

Calvin was extremely proud of Doug, and would often take him to see different people in the community. "He was a very good father," says Joyce. "He would wash Doug's diapers and he took him to Sydney to meet Aunt V." Although Doug was five when his father took him to visit the woman who raised Calvin, he says his memory always goes to the train ride with his father. "That was the first time I got to spend time alone with Dad," remembers Doug.

Wanting to spend more time at home and less time on the road, Calvin attempted to find a job in Halifax. He approached grocery stores and dry cleaning businesses to see if he could act as their deliveryman, but the consensus was that no one wanted a Black man delivering to their homes. He soon realized that being self-employed would be the only way to make some money. He began by selling coal and wood with a man named Charlie Durant. Charlie eventually bought a convenience store on Creighton Street, which sold groceries and household products. Calvin continued to sell coal and wood to several communities until Charlie moved to Montreal and needed someone to take over the store. Calvin ran the business until he decided he was no longer content living in his current neighbourhood and would have to relocate to another city to find a home for his growing family.

On January 21, 1953, the Rucks welcomed their second child into the world. Their daughter, Rochelle, was born at the Grace Maternity in Halifax.

Calvin didn't want to raise his children in a small apartment. He wanted a house. But finding someone to rent to a Black couple was easier said than done. Joyce can recall the discrimination Blacks experienced when it came to the communities they lived in and the homes they were able to have: "People would drive by the Black neighbourhood and say, 'Look how they live,' but they made you live that way – even the government. Gottingen Street used to be one of the busiest streets in Halifax. They've now taken away the banks and grocery stores on the street. They've all left and people just say look at them."

During his search, Calvin approached the Halifax Relief Commission, an organization that had been put in place following the Halifax Explosion in 1917. Among other responsibilities, the commission was implemented in 1918 to aid those who needed to rebuild after the disaster. The Hydrostone in north-end Halifax was built after the explosion and Calvin was hoping to claim one of these homes, but he quickly discovered this community had no plans of selling to Blacks.

There was no way they were going to get a house in Halifax, and as the Rucks found out, finding an apartment in the city was just as difficult. The search for a proper home took years, as landlords refused to do business with a Black man. Calvin made an attempt to gain support and sought help from the city by sharing his case of discrimination with the city's mayor. Uninterested, the mayor blatantly stated that "there was nothing he could do to help."

Despite the obvious barriers, Calvin wasn't relocating out of Halifax without first trying everything he could think of. He would call landlords and attempt to disguise his voice and change his last name to MacDonald to see if they would rent to him, but as soon as they found out the colour of his skin, he heard the same thing time and time again: they were not renting a decent apartment to a Black man, as they felt that those living in the area and those looking for places to live would be turned off from the neighbourhood. The couple was forced to either stay where they were in the north end of Halifax or journey across the Angus L. Macdonald Bridge to Dartmouth. The Rucks were determined not to be part of the status quo, so in 1955, with a five-year-old boy and two-year-old girl, they packed up their belongings to start a new life in Dartmouth.

Calvin found a man who was selling a building lot in the Westphal area of Dartmouth. Although he knew his family would be the only Black family in the neighbourhood, he liked the location, as it was close to schools and businesses.

It was not long before the buzz of a Black family wanting to move into this all-white neighbourhood began to travel through the Westphal community. The man who sold him the lot was also taking the heat as his entire family was now known as "nigger lovers." The residents, stating they did not want a Black family to reside in their neighbourhood, signed a petition. Their reasoning behind such dislike was that it was assumed the Rucks would build a substandard home that would not fit in among the others. The petition was sent to the county councillor, but nothing came of it, as Calvin was able to demonstrate to the councillor that his home was going to be just as good as his neighbours' dwellings.

Although the purpose of the Ruck family moving to Dartmouth and buying a home was to have a better life for their children, Joyce admits she felt more comfortable bringing her children up in Halifax, in a predominantly Black neighbourhood, than in an area where Blacks were seen as an inadequate and an inferior race. The family was constantly reminded that they were not welcome. Letters were cut out of magazines and newspapers and pasted together to create anonymous hate mail.

"I remember one in particular that consisted of various letters and words cut from magazines and glued to the page," says Doug. "It made a few nasty comments and made reference to niggers. I have no idea if Dad ever raised any of this with the police or simply felt it was of little value to do so."

Rochelle, Martin, Doug and Calvin on the front steps of 27 Walker Street, 1964.

Phone calls were coming in declaring the dislike the community had for this family they barely knew. Such intense opposition was wasted on the family, however, as Joyce and Calvin were determined to make it work at 27 Walker Street. The couple explained to their children the struggles they would have to face, and as the Ruck children started interacting with other neighbourhood children, they began to see how they were different from their playmates. One particular instance stands out: a young boy told Joyce his parents told him that if he continued to play with these children he would "turn" Black. Despite his parents' cautionary tale, the young boy enjoyed playing with the Ruck children and continued spending time with them, without any drastic colour changes to report.

Calvin at 27 Walker Street about 1995.

Such an anecdote is mild when it came to how children handled interacting with peers of a different colour. When the Rucks first moved to the area, Martin, their youngest, had not yet been born, and Doug, being the eldest, quickly learned that he would have to fight his way through school. Although he was fighting more than he ever did in Halifax, he wasn't scared of these children. They weren't like the children in Halifax.

"I wasn't as afraid of the kids in Dartmouth because I knew if I had to, I could properly defend myself. I wasn't scared because I didn't see them as being as tough as the kids in Halifax. They appeared softer, and gentler. Even though they were mean, they didn't talk as harshly. The kids in Halifax were really poor and grew up tough. They survived by being tough. They would get their money for lunch by taking it from other kids."

Doug sparring with Calvin.

When they were very young, Calvin taught both of his sons how to box. It was a very basic teaching, but he knew, unfortunately, that it would be useful. Unlike the adults in the neighbourhood, children were not as subtle or tactful when it came to their hatred towards someone who wasn't like themselves. Doug was fighting almost every day. As soon as a boy would approach him, he would remember what he was taught and quickly get into his boxing stance. Such preparedness threw the other boys off, as they were ready to wrestle this boy to the ground and knew nothing of boxing. Upon assuming his boxing stance, Doug always had one goal going into a fight: to ensure that he hurt his opponent enough so they wouldn't attack him again. And thanks to his boxing lessons, he achieved that goal.

"The fights didn't last long," says Doug, adding that after punching a kid in the nose or the head, the fight would be over. "The school didn't really have to break it up because the fight would end pretty quickly."

Fighting became routine for Doug. In the morning, at recess, lunch, after school or in the hallways, someone was always looking to torment him. Doug recalls not being able to get to the washroom without someone finding him and pushing him around. Like his father, Doug was proud and he too had a point to prove in that community.

One particular day at recess, a boy who was bigger than Doug attacked him from behind and held him to the ground for the entire recess period. Doug was unable to move. After recess, as the kids went back into the school, Doug couldn't stand the idea that someone had defeated him and made him look weak. It bothered him to the point that as soon as the children entered the coatroom, Doug attacked that same boy and threw him across the floor. "I couldn't allow him to think he had an advantage, or anyone else to think he had an advantage. I just couldn't afford that."

Doug wasn't only protecting himself. He had a younger sister who was putting up with the same treatment he was; not to the same extent, but the teasing and tormenting still followed her every day. As an older brother, he wanted to protect his sister, so as soon as he heard that two boys were bothering Rochelle, he found them, fought them, and put enough fear into them to ensure they would never harass his baby sister again.

In the early 1960s, children from Cherry Brook began being bused to schools in Dartmouth. More Black students began coming to the once predominantly white schools, but until then, the Ruck kids were singled out and were reminded of their differences daily.

"I got tired of the fighting," says Doug. "I wasn't a child that wanted to fight, but I was always ready and eventually I came to accept that it was something I had to do."

Although Doug grew weary of constantly having to defend himself, he made sure his opponent never became wise to how he was feeling inside. "Kids who I fought would get older kids to come after me. One day as I was coming back from the store to get bread, this big guy came to get me. I think he shaved," Doug recalls with a laugh. "He threw me in the ditch five or six times and I just kept coming back at him. Then he threw me in again. There was no way I could beat him, but I wasn't going to stay down there. Eventually he got tired and stopped and left. I picked up my squashed bread and went home."

Calvin was strict with his children, but Doug never worried about getting into trouble with his parents when it came to the fighting. He never started the altercations, and Joyce and Calvin understood it was something he had to do. The children understood that when they were chastised or apprehended for their behaviour, it was for valid reasons. Calvin taught his children early on that because of their race they would be quickly judged and assumptions would be made about their behaviour. He was extremely committed to seeing that his children were always mannerly and respectful, because he knew the impact it would have on them if they were seen as rude or ignorant children. He knew that living in an entirely white neighbourhood where they were not wanted meant that his children were being judged solely on the colour of their skin and it was just assumed that they would be troublemakers. His children understood this too and remembered it wherever they went.

Across the Macdonald Bridge, Calvin's brother Art was raising a family of his own. Calvin's nephew, Darren Ruck, recalls also dealing with racism, but not only from his fellow classmates.

"My dad and Uncle Calvin wouldn't allow us to use racism as an excuse for not doing well in school. When I said I didn't get a good mark in math because my teacher's a racist, they would just say go upstairs and do your homework. But at the same time, if he thought there was some truth in my story, he would go and check it out. He wouldn't necessarily give me the benefit of knowing that he checked it out. My job was to do the homework. His job was to check out my story. He didn't want to mix the two.

"There was so much of it [racism] that you became numb to it. I remember a teacher calling me once a Black Santa Claus. There's nothing you can do but laugh it off 'cause you're there being humiliated publicly in front of your classmates."

While his opponents were numerous, Doug says one person he never fought was Scott Sanford. The boys met in primary. "Scott was tough," says Doug. But that didn't stop their peers from picking on Doug, and Scott by association. Walking down the street together was a sight to be seen, as people would yell from their cars "nigger" to Doug and "nigger lover" to Scott. But Scott didn't care and the two remain close friends to this day. "A lot of kids were intrigued or fascinated with kids that were different," says Doug. "I think it was mostly the parents that instilled in them a fear or dislike."

On January 26, 1959, Calvin and Joyce expanded their family with the birth of their son, Martin. By the time the youngest Ruck went off to school in 1964, the racial tension was not as great. "Doug fought a lot of the early battles," says Martin. "I tended to use humour rather than my fists to deal with stupidity. And we were more established in the neighbourhood by then."

Halifax Regional Municipality mayor Michael Savage, son of the former Dartmouth mayor and premier of Nova Scotia Dr. John Savage, spent a lot of time with Martin throughout their school years and recalls his humour. "There weren't many Black kids in the school. He was the class clown. He would say anything to anybody. I remember one time the teacher was yelling at him and he said, 'I know, I know, I'm the Black sheep of the classroom.' He was just always the guy that wanted to make fun."

While parents were hesitant to allow their children to spend time around the Ruck children, Calvin decided to make them an offer that some kids couldn't refuse. Just like he used to do on Tupper Street with his brother Winston, once the months turned colder, Calvin would make an ice rink in his backyard. "This broke down racial barriers in the neighbourhood," remarks Doug.

Mike Savage also grew up in Westphal and can recall spending time at the Ruck rink with Martin. "I remember one year he built this rink and we went and played hockey there."

Before the snow would fall, Calvin would set out the form for the rink. Once it started to snow he would begin to pat the snow down, making sure it was packed firm, and then continue flooding throughout the winter. He built boards around the ice pad and each year the construction was a little more elaborate than the year before.

"He built up a thick layer of ice and he worked on it every single night," recalls Doug. "In the spring, the ice was probably the last thing to melt because it was so thick. He eventually put seats and benches as part of the sides so you could sit down and put your skates and things on. Spring would come and he would dismantle it and put the boards off to the side and as soon as the fall came around he would start building things up again. Each year he always improved it, making it bigger and better. By the time it was finished it covered a fair bit of the backyard, so you could have a fair number of kids on it skating and playing hockey."

Calvin also increased the wattage of the outdoor lights so the rink could be used at night.

"Dad was a good skater," says Doug. "He would show me how to do different things. He had a nice smooth stride when he was skating."

Mike Savage's hockey memories also go back to the Russia-Canada hockey series of 1972, which he watched at the Ruck household. "I spent the night at Martin's house and we watched the hockey game with his family. It's kind of cool. I was always a little bit in awe of his father."

The Ruck children had a great respect for their father and they learned more from what he did than what he said.

"Calvin said so many people have so much to say and talk about but never do anything – he wanted people to make things happen, not just talk about it," says Calvin's colleague Mike Tynes.

Calvin had several opportunities to play the victim or lash out at those who treated him as inferior, but he never did. He remained focused, knowing he would gain respect from being the bigger man, and stayed consistent in his fight for civil rights.

"He was punctual, fastidious, persevering, in what he undertook to do," says colleague, author and historian Dr. Bridglal Pachai. "He never kept one waiting when he made a promise to do something. I remember him as an example of a person who never put off for tomorrow what could be done today. And I saw that because I tried to live my life that way."

After moving to Westphal, Joyce's nerves became overactive, and with Calvin still working as a car porter on the railroad part-time, she was left alone with the children in a neighbourhood where she was unwanted and disliked. One week she became very ill and managed to contact Calvin on the road. Upon his return home, the couple went to the doctor and it was decided that it was not safe for Joyce to be alone. Calvin also felt that it was not fair to leave his wife for days at a time to care for the children

Rochelle, Calvin, Martin, Joyce, and Doug, Christmas 1959.

by herself, so he decided to take a few months off to stay home with his family. This meant Calvin had to look for another job in the community.

He was a man of many hats, constantly entering into new ventures as well as continuing to support and strengthen the ones he had started years before. Calvin contacted a manager at a local grocery store and asked if he could make their deliveries. Before he was hired on, Calvin went through a unique, not to mention race-specific, interviewing process – he was asked to clean the windows in the back room (an odd task to test one's delivery skills). When Calvin entered the room, he noticed there was money on the windowsill, but thought nothing of it. About fifteen minutes into the job, the manager came in to check on Calvin as well as his money on the windowsill. Calvin soon realized that he was not only being scored on his window-cleaning ability. When the manager saw the money was still there, he told Calvin he could stop cleaning and that he had gotten the job. Calvin stayed at the grocery store until he found better work that would allow him to leave the railroad completely and stay in Nova Scotia permanently.

During the 1960s, Calvin was juggling several jobs. He would wake up early in the morning and head down to the Bank of Montreal in Shearwater to perform janitorial duties. He would then take care of maintenance and cleaning at CFB Shearwater, located on the eastern shore of Halifax harbour. He worked specifically in the library and made it a goal to read every book in the building. He was constantly learning new things and every week when the magazines were thrown out, he would bring them home and read every single one of them.

While performing his duties at the base, Calvin's eyes were drawn to a group of young air cadets who had been selected from across Canada to participate in a training program. Lieutenant-Colonel (retired) Robert Maxwell was one of those young men and was the only Black cadet selected for the program. Calvin introduced himself to the young cadet. "I was impressed with the man right away," says Maxwell, "as he had a presence about him. At the time, he was a cleaner, but from his manner and bearing, I thought he was a teacher." This chance meeting led to a lifelong friendship. "My views of him never wavered, but became even stronger over the years as I got to know him better."

When Calvin took on extra cleaning duties, Doug and Martin would come along and help with the work. "At least once or twice a year all the mess floors would have to be stripped of the old wax that had built up and fresh wax applied. I remember that whatever cleaning substances he would use would actually hiss and bubble in the bucket and would make your eyes water. The mixture was truly noxious and we never wore any kind of mask or respirator."

Calvin did whatever he had to do to provide for his family. When he saw a void in a community he would try to fill it, while also making a profit, although not very large, for his family.

With Calvin having such late evenings, it was hard for Joyce to sleep until she knew her husband was safely home. She would sit up and wait for him with Doug, who would run into their bedroom and look out the window to see if car lights were coming down the street. "I always knew where he was," says Joyce. "He always called me if he was going somewhere or was going to be late."

It was normal to the Ruck children that their father worked so much. They actually found it strange when they would visit a friend's house and see a man at home, relaxing and reading the paper at five or six in the evening. A regular day for Calvin would sometimes end at midnight. Perhaps one of the secrets behind his stamina and energy was his ability to take his famous ten-minute naps. "He could maybe rest for ten minutes, close his eyes, tell Mom to wake him up in ten minutes and then go to a meeting that night," recalls Doug. "It was almost recreational. He worked to relax and then he relaxed to work. He did it all the time."

Calvin taught his children that you had to work hard for what you got and to never expect a handout. He never felt something should be given if you didn't deserve it. Therefore, he saw working long hours and weekends as something he had to do, to establish a quality of life for his children and grandchildren, so they didn't have to work quite the same way.

"My childhood was very different from my father's childhood," says Doug's daughter Jacqueline, "and the battles that I had to fight were different from the ones my grandfather had to fight because he already fought them successfully. And I have been the beneficiary of his struggles."

Despite the roadblocks and hatred he experienced in Dartmouth, Calvin knew it was God's plan for them to be in that city. He would describe his move to Dartmouth as "the best thing that ever happened." He had a love for Dartmouth and a love for its people, and he was determined to be the change the city needed.

"I think that Calvin Ruck is a real Dartmouth hero for what he went through and what he did in the neighbourhood," says Mike Savage. "And that perseverance and that commitment to social justice – just by being there, not by being difficult, but by being there doing what's right – that's pretty significant."

With a new job opportunity in the works, Calvin would soon achieve things that others viewed as impossible because of the colour of his skin, and this new opportunity would be the catalyst that would drive his passion for change.

The Westphal community was not just getting a Black man, they were getting an activist, a visionary, and a man who would ensure he would not leave that city as it was, whether everyone agreed with him or not.

3: Rising Above

About five miles west of Dartmouth, road signs direct you to the community of Preston. As you travel down winding roads, homes big and small will appear through the trees. Some of these are spaced considerably apart while others have been built with two, three or sometimes four homes on one large lot of land. The land is owned by one family while each home is owned by a different family member. During the War of 1812, thousands of Black Refugees fled to Canada, and many settled in Nova Scotia. It is their descendants who mostly make up the community of Preston today.

Calvin's home away from home was North and East Preston, Lake Loon and Cherry Brook, and his love for these communities, which collectively hold the largest percentage of Canadian-born Black people of any area in the country, was boundless.

Growing up I would hear of Preston and visit the area for different functions and get-togethers, but I never truly understood why Calvin had such strong ties to the area until I went back to conduct the interviews for this book. Being welcomed into people's homes with open arms and staying for hours, I realized that what brought Calvin back day in and day out were the faces. When I mentioned Calvin's name, these faces lit up and the stories just began to flow. These faces represent a legacy of his life. They represent the outcome of hard work and determination. They tell stories that will never be forgotten because lives were changed and dreams were achieved. Growing up, I wasn't able to put a face to the names Calvin spoke of, but now, these faces will stay in my mind and heart forever. They were Calvin's family and I now feel they are mine. I am grateful for the time I had with each of these individuals and while the anecdotes varied, they all began with one memory.

"I remember he used to come into the community with the dry cleaning," recalls Dr. Wanda Thomas Bernard, an Order of Canada recipient who has had a distinguished career in social work and who first met Calvin as a young girl. Wanda paints a picture of a man slowly driving down the winding gravel roads in an old panel truck.

"These were utility vehicles that were generally used by companies as delivery vans," explains Doug. "He had a sign company make up Deluxe Dry Cleaners signs with suction cups that he could put on the side of the truck when on his route. He also had metal rods placed inside the truck suspended from the ceiling so he could hang the clothes up. Dad had at least two or three trucks and then switched to station wagons. The trucks often broke down as they were used with a fair number of miles on them. None of the roads were paved so the trucks took quite a beating, especially in the spring when the roads were basically muddy paths full of ruts."

Many a time, if you saw the car go by, you may also spot a young boy in the passenger seat, gazing at the now familiar roads and homes. As the eldest boy, Doug was often called upon to help his father with his various business ventures and at a very young age he understood that the work his father was doing was not only to provide for his family, but also to provide for a community that had been denied these basic services.

"He was always aware of the local Black communities and very interested in promoting improved living conditions by, at least initially, providing basic services that other communities took for granted," explains Doug. "Mixed with this was also the fact that Dad was very concerned about providing for his own family and the dry cleaning business gave him a chance to address both concerns. Apparently Deluxe Dry Cleaners of Dartmouth had had a driver who briefly serviced Preston but it was short-lived. For Dad it was a part-time job that could supplement his regular full-time work, but more importantly an opportunity to bring something to the community they did not have.

There were those who seemingly believed that Blacks would not be interested in paying to have their clothes cleaned, but the growth of Dad's dry cleaning route showed such was not the case and the people of the community were concerned about cleanliness and willing to pay for it. Dad had to convince the dry cleaning company that this was a viable enterprise."

While dry cleaning was the initial service offered, his visits usually amounted to so much more. "I don't remember us having much need for dry cleaning," Wanda recalls. "I just remember the conversations. He was always checking in. 'How are you? What's going on? What are your interests?' He was always so pleasant and he always seemed to be offering something, whether it was the dry cleaning or information or whatever."

"I met Mr. Ruck when I was a little girl," explains Dr. Carolyn Thomas. "He used to come to the house and if people wanted to leave laundry, he would pick it up. It seemed like I always knew him. 'Oh, here's Mr. Ruck! Mom, Mr. Ruck's here!' He was always here."

So how did a man who had no previous connections become, as Carolyn puts it, "a fixture in the community"? Calvin used the dry cleaning as an ice breaker for his further involvement in East and North Preston, Cherry Brook and Lake Loon.

"Very few did that," says Marilyn Smith. "He didn't need to come here." Marilyn and Roger Smith have lived in East Preston all their lives and their third-generation home was built by Marilyn's grandfather. The house has seen many renovations since that first structure stood decades ago, but the memories have survived through each upgrade.

"Calvin and Joyce used to come here in this house. Most of the time he was here talking to my mother after hours because she worked during the day."

One of Calvin's most popular business ventures was his seasonal school supplies sale. A majority of the Black families in these communities were unable to afford the proper school supplies for their children. At the beginning of every school year, Calvin would buy pencils, erasers, notebooks, pens and any other necessary supplies that were needed at a wholesale price, and travel through the community with Doug, selling the supplies for a cheaper price. While Calvin would deliver the dry cleaning, Doug would be at the back of the truck, selling supplies to anyone who was interested. That business eventually grew to include Halloween and Christmas candy.

"Everybody waited for Mr. Ruck on Saturday to buy school supplies for their kids," says Dolly Williams. "Especially during August. They would go to town on Saturday and if they weren't home they would leave a note for Mr. Ruck saying what they needed. Just like going to a store.

"I remember one day, he wanted to know where somebody lived," she adds, "and I went with him to show him and the woman didn't have any money so he let her have the stuff. It was his business, but it wasn't about the money, it was about people. He was about the moral principles and helping the fellow man."

Although not his specific title at the time, Calvin was getting the reputation of a social activist through the conversations he had with those in the Black communities while carrying out his many entrepreneurial jobs.

"As I was researching on the Black community, I went often to the Preston area and met with members of the various communities – North Preston, East Preston, Cherry Brook, Lake Loon – and came to know of his involvement in the communities there," recalls Bridglal Pachai. "There were social workers in the community and Calvin stood out."

About 1968, a man in Halifax received word of Calvin's efforts and decided that if he was already doing the work, then he might as well have an office and an official title to go along with it. H.A.J. (Gus) Wedderburn, an educator turned lawyer and strong advocate of equality for the disadvantaged, approached Calvin about a job as a community development officer. With a grade ten education and a new title after his name, Calvin now had a license to actively work within the community and be the change he wanted to be. It didn't take long for Calvin to strengthen relationships with the people of these communities, making his new role a natural and smooth transition. "He was doing community development when he was doing the dry cleaning," says Wanda.

Wanda's family was left to pick up the pieces after losing her father in a car accident. "For me, my father's death was probably a seminal moment in time because my mother had so many children. She had ten children of her own, plus she was raising two of her grandchildren and her oldest child was eighteen and the youngest was eighteen months old.

I was in the middle. I was twelve and my sister Val was fourteen. It seems to me that a lot of people started looking out for Momma after that and Calvin was one of those people."

Calvin was also looking out for the youth of the community. "I remember when he started the youth group," recalls Wanda with a smile. Wanda's original desire to join the youth group was because her big sister Val was a part of it. As she reminisces about times spent with her sister, she becomes emotional. "To me she was larger than life. She died ten years ago, but I still miss her like it was yesterday. If Val was doing something I thought was interesting, I would tag along. And so I was always hanging out with her and her friends. I was shy and reserved. When she said she was joining the youth group, I thought, 'Okay, sounds interesting. I guess I'll go along.' They made me the secretary. Probably because I didn't say a lot. And I remember Mr. Ruck saying, 'Wanda is always so quiet.' But really, a person who's taking notes should be quiet, because you have to be a good listener."

Wanda is not the only one who speaks proudly of the duties Calvin assigned to them. "Mr. Ruck had an office in the basement of the daycare centre and the daycare centre was just getting started," explains Roger Smith. "He hired five or six of us as painters to go in and paint these homes. So we would go in and do the painting day in and day out. But then one day he came to me and he said, 'Listen, how would you like to do something else?' He said, 'I need somebody in the office to answer the phone and take messages for me.' So he saw something in me other than being a painter. So I stayed in the office all day and twiddled my thumbs and got any messages that came in while the other guys were out painting. I just love painting today because of that," Roger adds with a laugh.

Marilyn Smith says Calvin's ability to discover skills in young people was innate. "He had a gift to see qualities in people and that wasn't something you learned, it was something that came very naturally to him. He was a very good judge of character. I would say everyone he took under his wing accomplished something and he was very proud of that. He played that father figure for a lot of youth. He's playing Dad to all of these kids and still raising a great family, so that speaks volumes."

The youth group would also prove to be a stepping stone for many of these kids. And while Calvin was already aware of their potential, he made sure others outside of the community knew it as well. Always keeping his ear to the ground, the newly appointed community development officer kept track of who was hiring throughout the city and made sure these young people had a chance to apply. At that time, it was a foreign concept to put a Black male or female on the payroll, but to Calvin, it just made sense and he wasn't going to rest until he saw it accomplished.

"My oldest sister Betty was the first person from this community to work in a store in downtown Dartmouth, and he made that happen," explains Wanda. "It was Stedmans. He wanted to change the face of the business community in Dartmouth, so part of his strategy was to find people in the community that he could put into the position to apply for different jobs. I think he obviously would have worked with Betty to get her prepared to go for that job and she got it. She was the first person of African descent to work in a store in downtown Dartmouth. That was written up in *The Chronicle Herald*.

"It's no wonder he ended up working in human rights 'cause he always worked from a rights perspective," adds Wanda. "He wasn't going to send someone down there who wouldn't do a good job. If you're representing, you're representing."

"It was a major breakthrough," says Doug. "To actually have someone approach Mr. Stedman himself was a big deal in itself. What he put to him was that if you expect these people to continue to shop in this store and receive their money, then you better start employing them. Stedman, being a businessman, saw there may be a chance that he would actually lose revenue and Dad picking Betty was a thing of knowing someone who would meet the challenge. Not just do the job, but deal with some pushback. One thing Dad always referred to was Jackie Robinson going into Major League Baseball. He would say, 'You're going to have people saying nasty things to you, but you're going to remain dignified, you're going to be at work on time every day, you're going to dress properly.' He would nurture and foster those individuals."

One of the most memorable employment opportunities was a multiple hiring in Dartmouth in the late 1960s. Kmart, one of the largest retail chains at that time, was opening a new location in the city, which meant several new jobs would be opened up to the neighbourhood. Unfortunately, these employment opportunities were only directed towards those in the white communities, something Calvin was not willing to accept as the bottom line, so he paid a visit to the hiring committee. Through reason and conversation, six Black girls were hired to be associates at the Dartmouth location.

Terri Gray, a retired nurse, was fifteen when she was hired as a part-time sales associate at the Tacoma Drive store. Terri's mother and father were Calvin and Joyce's best friends, and she recalls going to several interviews for different positions that had been arranged by Calvin.

"He was always after me about employment," she recalls. "He suggested that I go and I get part-time work at Kmart. I was petrified. I was always very shy anyways so that didn't help. But he was confident that with my intelligence and the way I carried myself, I remember him saying there shouldn't be a problem and if there was a problem to let him know. I think it was done before I even got there. I think I just had to show up."

The news of minority workers travelled fast and the grand opening for the new store had much more excitement and hype than originally expected. Calvin, Joyce and their three children all went to opening day and as Joyce recalls, Calvin showed his thanks for the six hires with his wallet. "He bought so many things that day. Things he would never use!" This one store created a domino effect in the neighbourhood and soon after, Calvin had other employers calling him to find out if other Black men and women were in need of employment.

"He would say if Terri doesn't get this there's a problem," says Doug. "Everybody shopped at the same stores but no one who was Black was hired at those stores. Dad said this is wrong and took it on himself. First he found the stores and then he went out and found the people. If someone couldn't get there, he would drive them and wait outside to see how it went. It was extraordinary."

While being hired in a predominantly white workforce was a major step forward for the Black community, the superior mentality among whites was still apparent. More Black staff meant the potential for more

Black customers and not everyone was necessarily comfortable with their new clientele.

"When I worked at the Dominion Store on Canal Street, the head cashier had a few biases of her own," says Terri, "and I think she was very watchful and especially watchful when a lot of the people from the country would come into that store. She would hover a little bit. She never really said anything to me, but I was just conscious of her being around."

The rewards were great for these young kids who were just starting to see their own potential. Hard work deserved hard play and Calvin made sure they were reaping the benefits of their labour. But nothing was going to just be handed to them. They had to earn it.

"Up until Mr. Ruck came, we played stick ball in the road," recalls Roger Smith. "Hit the ball, wherever the ball stopped, walk to that point, hit the ball again. If a car came, we yelled, 'Car.' He saw that and said, 'No, you need to get organized. You need to have a ball field.' So we had tag days." As Roger continues to tell the story of the countless hours standing outside of Sobeys and liquor stores with a small can, he begins to laugh. "Every May there were tag days. We would raise money for uniforms, balls, bats – whatever we needed. I think [Calvin] collected more money than anyone."

Calvin also wanted to share his love of hockey with these communities. "That was the first time we had indoor hockey," says Gary Johnson, who took part in many of Calvin's groups and programs, "and guess who our first ref on the ice was? He was! He got ice for us and he was a ref for us. We organized a league between Preston, Halifax, Dartmouth and Cherry Brook. That was the first Black hockey league."

"If truth be told," adds Marilyn Smith, "I don't think we would be as developed as we are without Calvin. Because those simple things that Roger was talking about, that became a bigger fundraiser. So he taught us how to do the fundraising and people are still doing things like that. Those simple things he taught."

4: Pushing Past The City Lines

While Calvin emphasized the importance of community, he was also on a mission to broaden young minds and create new experiences for these youth. Some had never been farther than their own neighbourhood limits. There was a whole world that existed across the bridge and it was called Halifax.

"He really wanted us as young people to know that there was life outside of Preston," says Wanda Thomas Bernard. "And for many of us, we didn't know that. We weren't getting on a bus and going into town. There were no buses. My mother was working, doing domestic work and then on the weekend she would go shopping. She tended to take the children that were less well-behaved. I wasn't one of them so I didn't get to go into town."

Besides racial lines, Marilyn Smith says social lines were also drawn between Blacks of different parts of the city. "There was always this kind of stigma between Blacks from the city and from the Prestons," she explains. "It's still there. Almost like we were just uneducated; like we just weren't on their level. But Mr. Ruck always came around to try to expose us to those things, to take us through the city. He used to come out and take us on bus trips to the NSAACP [Nova Scotia Association for the Advancement of Coloured People] meetings and half the time I think I was going just to get out of the community."

Dr. Bridglal Pachai says this division among Black communities is apparent throughout the country. "The Black community in Nova Scotia in particular, and I think in Canada, is a divided one. Terribly divided. Those who came from Africa have a place, those who came from the Caribbean have a place, those who came from the U.K. have a place and so on. It's a matter of selective membership, not gracious and spontaneous membership. Very selective. Those who derived their ancestry from the islands were particularly treated as a group – those who came from Barbados, for example. The late Gus Wedderburn used to tell me over and over and over again, he said, 'Man, this thing here, never mind what we do, we don't belong.' And somehow, somewhere, I believe Calvin was troubled by this. Why do we fragment ourselves? Why can't we move along together?"

Calvin chose to ignore these invisible lines of division and moved forward with his plans to bridge the gap between the people of North and East Preston, Cherry Brook and Lake Loon with the rest of the city.

"The most backward thing at certain times is this fragmentation of the community," adds Dr. Pachai. "Who is indigenous and who is not. The word indigenous is a plague in Nova Scotia. I have always opposed it. By what virtue is anyone indigenous? How would a descendant of a Black Loyalist and a Black Refugee be considered an indigenous person and a descendant from the Caribbean be considered an outsider? But that is how it has been. And I think that that was one of the roadblocks to advancement in Nova Scotia and I don't think Calvin was ever a part of that."

Now an organized group, the officially titled Youth on the Move was living up to its name. With several youth movements taking place in Halifax, Calvin made sure the Preston communities were well represented. But these field trips didn't just stop in Halifax.

When people became involved in something, the first link always seemed to be Calvin. Some of the ideas may have seemed far-fetched or foreign to these small communities, but for Calvin, if other people were doing things then why couldn't they? One of those people who found herself in charge of one of Calvin's random ideas was Dolly Williams.

"He said, 'I know a young lady that does majorettes and I got her to come out and do it dirt cheap. The East Preston Majorettes we'll call it.' We went down to Lunenburg and that was our first major trip."

While Calvin had Dolly and the community excited about this new group, it proved more of a challenge to receive the same reception from the towns hosting the parades. At their first appearance, the CBC personnel refused to film these young, eager girls of the East Preston Majorettes.

"They had nice blue sparkling outfits. They looked great. Sharp. And they got a lot of claps, but they took the cameras off of us and Calvin said, 'Ignore them, just keep going.' We got a lot of applause."

While it may have taken some a bit of time to warm up to the idea of an interracial parade, the girls in the blue sparkling outfits began to receive requests to appear at parades all over Atlantic Canada, and Calvin made sure this group of twenty-five to thirty girls would be there.

"He took us to Middle Musquodoboit. Wherever he went, if there was a parade, exhibition, if he knew about it, we went. When we went out into the broader community and did the parades, people were shocked that we had a white instructor and the Black parents coming beside. We told the kids when you go, if there's name-calling, ignore them, just keep marching.

"And every year they looked for us. If they couldn't get a hold of us, they would call Mr. Ruck. And when we got there, Calvin made sure we had a good spot and that they weren't putting us at the end of the parade. We were always near a band. Calvin made sure that we had music.

"The kids loved it. Every Saturday we had rehearsal. They practised in the hall, on the back roads, out there marching. He gave those kids a lot of self-esteem. And from that my daughters went into tap dancing, they went into baseball, but the first was doing the majorettes and they weren't afraid to compete. It taught the kids to go out and compete."

Carolyn Thomas also recalls when Calvin shared an idea with the Recreation Association, a committee Carolyn was president of at the time. "He had this vision of a band, a Preston youth band. He wanted trumpets. Everything Stadacona or Shearwater [military bands] had, he wanted here. 'Cause he saw the natural and raw talents in these young people. He would say 'Carolyn, we can do this.' And I'm saying, 'Yeah, let's do this,' and I'm very pregnant with my last child at forty-one years. And I'm sitting up there at this big community meeting and he's saying what this is all about, and all of a sudden I feel this water and I feel this pain and they had to take me from there as I'm sitting there with Mr. Ruck."

From painting homes to marching in parades, it was the little things that made the difference for this younger generation. Calvin's focus on them did not go unnoticed and although many say they didn't see it then, they realized in later years the great impact he had on their lives.

"With a lot of children, Mr. Ruck was the lifeline," says Marilyn Smith, who works for the Halifax Regional Municipality. "You knew you were cared for [by your own family], but that person to guide you – he filled that role for so many different people. He threw a lifeline to a lot of people. He helped people with resumés. He was a jack of all trades. If we had that kind of an individual now … so many of our kids could use that now. I wouldn't say sacrifices because his family was intact through all of it, but sacrifices to the degree of an impact on his own time, his personal time. He gave that up to come here and help someone. That's why we can appreciate it. We had one man that had that impact on all of us."

"I think he was an adult who listened to young people," says Wanda Thomas Bernard. "And there weren't many adults in the community that listened to young people. We were fortunate we had a few. When Mr. Ruck came around, he was one of those adults that made the young people feel important. Like we had a voice."

"Personally, growing up, the father figure for me was my granddad, but outside of this environment, if I had to pick somebody, it would be Mr. Ruck," says Marilyn. "His approach was not one of an adult versus a kid. He bridged the gap a little bit and had a great tolerance for us. I can never remember him ever raising his voice. There was a respect for him that people just automatically gave."

Calvin was inspiring a young generation to rise up and be the change in their communities, and while many applauded the efforts, there were those who were concerned with the platform these youth were being given.

"Some of the adults were still in their old ways," recalls Gary Johnson. "They were always criticizing the young folks. They didn't want changes. They called us the Black Power. They thought we were starting a

Black Power group because we wanted telephones, we wanted paved roads. Some people appreciated it, but he still had enemies."

Calvin had now grown accustomed to dealing with opposition, but most would come from another race. This opposition had nothing to do with race. A fear of change was standing in Calvin's way.

"I think some of the older folks were a bit timid," says colleague and friend Wayne Adams, a former city councillor and the first Black person elected to the Nova Scotia legislature. "They were afraid. People hadn't gone those places before; they hadn't made those statements before. It was a new frontier. But we were excited as kids."

Wayne understood firsthand this fear of change. In 1972, Wayne started a program called *Black Journal* on CHNS radio with the focus of racial equality. Getting guests on the show was no easy feat as many were afraid to lend their voice. "People thought I was a radical," he explains. "A lot of people were afraid to go on the radio, but Calvin was one of the willing participants in the early days. After he and Gus [Wedderburn] and a few others started participating, people started getting more comfortable and it became a very popular program. We got two national awards for it."

Calvin's excitement for change was unstoppable, and he was determined to break that barrier and allow progress to flow freely into these communities. "The community wouldn't be developed [if he hadn't come]," notes Gary. "We would still be way behind. He contributed to the way of thinking. We became a powerful youth group. The way he developed us as young people gave us the determination and know-how to go and start some of these projects ourselves."

Gary, who is the father of former world heavyweight contender Kirk Johnson and the longtime amateur coach of Olympian Custio Clayton, has trained fourteen national boxing champions, a world champion and two Olympians. He says his desire to mentor stemmed from Calvin's leadership when he was younger.

"The knowledge I got from Mr. Ruck contributed to that and he instilled leadership in us and showed us how to be leaders. Of all the leaders we got involved with, Mr. Ruck was the most influential one."

Calvin supported these young people in whatever way he could. He invited them to have their weekly meetings in a building known as the "teacherage." Prior to expanding to include a clinic and daycare, the two- to three-storey structure acted as a boarding house for teachers and was also used as Calvin's office.

"He was our counsellor and advisor," says Gary. "So after that, they couldn't really say anything because we had an adult that was our advisor. We began to invite people like Reverend [Donald] Skeir [who served as pastor for forty-plus years of East Preston United Church, Cherry Brook United Baptist Church and St. Thomas United Baptist Church] and Dr. John Savage, and we got involved in different things. They stopped calling us Black Power. Mr. Ruck made it possible that we had a drop-in centre. We converted his office into a health clinic. There were three communities he had to take care of. He was so busy."

This drop-in centre was open to anyone who wanted a place to hang out, talk, or just be amongst peers. "Mr. Ruck allowed me to bring in really young boys, ages nine to twelve. At that time they didn't have anything to do and parents didn't care where they wandered. We called it Le Garçon Club. We used a French word to make it different," Gary explains with a laugh.

Calvin's ability to bridge the generational gap was evident in not only how these kids were taking new pride in themselves because he said they were worth it, but also in how parents and youth alike felt safe in the presence of the Rucks.

"Over the years, as I grew older, I started going to Admiral Westphal School," says Carolyn Thomas. "You always knew, Mr. and Mrs. Ruck's house: 27 Walker Street. I'm in trouble; I'm running there, because they're safe. There are some parents who will tell you these are safe people or a safe home, but then there are people who you know intuitively that they are. And Mr. and Mrs. Ruck were those kinds of people."

"He had a caring spirit," adds Dolly Williams. "And that smile of his. I can't remember Calvin ever being upset with kids. I've never seen an angry side of him. He would say, 'You know, you need to think about this?' He always had a reason why you should think about it and do it. But never to the point that he would get irate with you. That was not Calvin. Compared to his big tall brother, the steelworker in the union, I would say, oh my goodness, what a difference. Calvin is so soft-spoken. His brother Winston was loud. Calvin was more like calming the waters."

Calvin took a different approach to discrimination and racism than perhaps other social activists might take. He saw no purpose in quarrelling or raising his voice, and at the end of the day he ensured his dignity always remained intact. "He was never confrontational," says Bridglal Pachai. "I think he just took it quietly and left it. Because he didn't want to add to the division. If you are going to quarrel amongst yourselves on a point like that, it's self-defeating. You gain a point and you lose a whole measure simply by fighting amongst yourselves. He didn't fight. But I know he felt it. If he didn't fight, he surely felt it."

Not wanting future generations to feel the pains of racism he experienced too often, Calvin proved to be exactly what the youth of these communities needed to push them towards brighter futures and motivate them to be the best they could be. And behind every conversation there was always one constant topic – education. "He was concerned about your education. It was a genuine interest," says Roger Smith.

While Calvin fully believed that anyone, no matter race or social status, could do whatever they wanted in life, he also stood firmly on the belief that education was the best tool to bettering one's situation in life.

"The conversation was always about what are your plans," recalls Wanda. "There was always a message about planning and preparing and thinking ahead. Education is really a tool to have a more promising future. When the opportunity became available for us to go to university, some of the work preparing us for that, it didn't come from the school, it came from people like Calvin."

The reality was, Black men and women were not expected by society to excel, were not expected to better themselves through their schooling and were certainly not expected to graduate at the top of their class. For many Black people, this way of thinking had been engrained since they were young and after seeing generation upon generation leaving school at an early age, they did not see the point of changing that pattern.

Darren Ruck describes his uncle Calvin as a mentor in his life, particularly when it came to the topic of education. "I went to visit him when he worked at the Nova Scotia Human Rights Commission and I was sort of stumbling around my career. I had come back from Toronto and was going to be an electronics engineer and that didn't really work out as well as I thought, so I came back to Halifax and started working for the dockyard in a very low-end job," he explains. "I met with him one day and he said basically, 'Darren, you need education. You need to take a course, go to community college, you need more than what you have now.' It was not long after that that I went back to university and interestingly enough I did quite well. The momentum began and I began to take it more seriously."

One of Calvin's favourite sayings was "The sky's the limit." There were no glass ceilings, there were no racial barriers and he wanted the youth of these communities to adopt this new, positive mindset.

"He gave us the enthusiasm to really stay in school because if it wasn't for him a lot of us would have dropped out of school," says Gary Johnson. "It got so that we made it a contest. Nobody wanted to fail. Everybody wanted to go on and get to at least grade twelve. He assisted our youth group in getting a bus to take people back and forth. That bus took us back and forth each day and it also took us to dances."

This was a new generation of achievers.

"That's what gets people, when you see a Black person who's educated," adds Dr. Henry Bishop, former curator of the Black Cultural Centre who describes Calvin as his role model and mentor. "He said that's what changes the whole persona of the culture – he would say the race. Our value of education has been tainted. We're seen as more valuable in entertainment and sports. The entertainment can go and sports can go but your education is still there. He said don't rely on those other things; once you get that education, you can get what you want. I wish more young people would think that way."

Calvin ensured his own children and grandchildren thought that way, putting a nugget about the importance of education into every interaction with his children. "I knew I was going to university even when I didn't know what you did at university," says Martin, an associate professor of psychology and urban education at the City University of New York. "Both he and Mom instilled that in us early on."

"As I got older, our main conversation was about education," says Calvin's granddaughter Jacqueline. "It almost always started with 'How is school going?' He was very proud when I was accepted into university and he would always say the sky's the limit in almost every conversation I had with him. As I got older, every conversation was more of an educational pep talk. Education was so important to him and it was important to him that his family be educated."

The concept of education also extended to learning about your neighbours, finding out about the places you were visiting and showing a genuine interest in those around you. Calvin wanted to learn more about people.

"When he went to Yarmouth, he would go to the library," says Doug's wife, Valerie Ruck. "He was always trying to find out more about the people wherever we went. When people came up to him he was always genuinely interested. If you talked to him, you knew he wasn't just going to say hi to you and that was it. He was genuinely interested in people."

Calvin also didn't put an age limit on education. "Mom went back to school, and again it was because of Mr. Ruck's encouragement," says Wanda. With a grade eight education, Wanda's mother enrolled in the adult education program, initiated by Calvin, and received her grade twelve diploma. "He wasn't only telling young people about the value of education," says Wanda. "He was doing that for older people as well."

As someone who completed his grade twelve equivalent in 1969, he was constantly learning and expanding his mind, taking advantage of courses at local community colleges and night schools. Between 1969 and 1977, Calvin received course credits in small business management, introductory and advanced sociology, public relations, paralegal, and Baptist history. "Calvin knew where every class was and what nights they were," says Dolly Williams.

Marilyn Smith was diagnosed with dyslexia at age thirty. She was working as a retail manager at a clothing store, and Calvin encouraged her do more. Marilyn enrolled in a two-year business course. "I was a young mother and a wife and enrolled in an accounting course."

Dolly and Sinclair Williams heard Calvin's thoughts on education many times over the years. As tears come to her eyes, Dolly recounts how education proved to make the difference in their lives.

"We had gotten married young and Sinclair was working to help build the Halifax Shopping Centre and then he got a job as maintenance at the hospital. Calvin was a social worker then, and I was doing housework and also working with Sardie's clothing manufacturing as a seamstress. Then I worked at the IWK as a ward assistant. Sinclair was at Camp Hill. Calvin approached both of us and said, 'You fellas should go back to high school and get your grade twelve.' He said it's not going to hurt anything and they have classes at Graham Creighton [school]. It was two nights a week, seven to nine p.m., and we went down and took our courses and got our grade twelve."

While Sinclair was still working at the hospital in the '70s, Calvin connected with another Roger Smith, the newly appointed chief of police. Roger had said he wanted to make the police department diverse. This was music to Calvin's ears and he wasted no time putting names forward.

"He went to one person at a time," says Valerie Ruck. "He had to talk them into believing in themselves. If he had a specific job that needed to be done, he would just pick a person and start talking to them quietly. He would plant a seed in them."

"Calvin went to Sinclair and Spencer Colley," says Dolly. "Sinclair said, 'No, Spencer can do it.' Calvin said, 'You know, Sinclair, you came through a lot, you've been blessed.' The one thing I liked about Calvin is he always talked about God. He said, 'God brought you this far for a reason. There's more in store for you and you need to take that chance and think about it.' I agreed with Calvin. I thought, a police officer? In Dartmouth? I said, 'Think about the money! I'm working at a hospital, we get union pay and also I get sick benefits.' I said, 'Do you really want to keep cleaning floors? This is an opportunity for you to be out there. You're very good with people.'"

After some thought and much convincing from his family, Sinclair decided to apply for the position. "He didn't wear the uniform until he was fully trained," explains Dolly. "On Dartmouth Natal Day they had him all ready and put him on Charmins' [a local store] corner on Prince Albert Road, doing the lights."

Seeing a Black policeman was a foreign concept for the people of Dartmouth, and it wasn't long before everyone was talking about it and wanting to see the sight for themselves. "People would say, 'Oh my gosh, there's a Black man there! A Black police officer!' He [Sinclair] was so excited," Dolly says proudly. "The kids were excited going downtown and seeing their dad in uniform. People said, 'I know that man, he's from East Preston!' That was his first display. Calvin initiated that. Calvin said to him, 'It's not going to be easy because people are prejudiced and there's a lot of racism going on, so you have to deal with that and you're going to be called names,' but he said, 'I know you can do it and I know you can handle it 'cause I know you.'"

While the community was excited about Sinclair's new position, Dolly says there were also those who saw this as an opportunity to take advantage of the law. "People said, 'We thought because he was Black he should be giving people a break.' But I said, 'White police officers don't do that so why would you expect it from this Black man?' So people got to realize this is his job, this is his income and they respected him for that."

The community was starting to see a change. "He taught, he mentored, he got things established, he got people to improve their homes, he created confidence in people, pride, he created leaders," says Marilyn. "When you stop and think about the impact, it's phenomenal."

While many welcomed these changes, there were a number of adversaries Calvin would have to deal with who were determined not to let this man turn their world upside down.

5: A House Is Not A Home

Housing was a significant issue in many of the predominantly Black communities. With little education on the matter and no drive to fight for what should have been rightfully theirs, many families were living in less than adequate conditions and paying for a home that was never lawfully theirs.

The root of the issue stems back to the early 1800s. During the War of 1812, approximately two thousand escaped slaves, later called the Black Refugees, arrived in Nova Scotia between 1813 and 1816. The two largest groups settled in Hammonds Plains and Preston. Upon their arrival, the government refused to grant them land. In 1816, those in Hammonds Plains received land grants of ten acres each, but the lots were of poor quality and they were prohibited from ever selling the land. Those in Preston were only granted warrants or licenses of occupation. In 1834, thirty men were granted six hundred acres in Hammonds Plains, and in 1842, those living in Preston received a grant of 1,800 acres, replacing the licenses of occupation issued in 1816.

"I was beginning as a younger person to become actively involved in the community," recounts Carolyn Thomas. "We have a tour business [that focuses on Black history and heritage] and one of the stories that I would always tell was how Mr. Ruck was offered the job when it became public news that the people in North Preston were living in terrible conditions."

Photos of pig barns with captions stating this is where these people lived hit the newspapers. A little-known community was now in the public eye. "The people turned it around and said, 'Well, we do live in poor conditions and if we're here, why is it like this?'" explains Carolyn. With a finger now pointed at it, the provincial government made a promise that something had and would change.

"Instead of the eyes being on the community, they became fixed on the government," continues Carolyn, "and even though they [those in the community] didn't call it that at the time, they were thinking institutional systemic racism."

The Nova Scotia Department of Social Services, now the Department of Community Services, hired Calvin to act as a social worker, but he knew he couldn't do it alone. "He was going to be the Mr. Fix It but he said, 'I can't do it by myself, it's a big problem,'" says Carolyn. "And they hired Eugene Williams as a second social worker. The two of them were there and action happened."

One couple, among many, who was directly affected by the concept of co-op housing was Dolly and Sinclair Williams. "We went to get a mortgage from the bank," begins Dolly, "and they wouldn't give us any money because they said people in Preston don't sell their homes so we don't give mortgages out there. There were all kinds of excuses. So Calvin knew about co-op housing so he came and sat down with me and Sinclair. We said we need a house. He said, 'If you can get five people with land, then we can get a co-op going.'

"We got the group formed and made sure we had all the money paid at a certain time. It was really reasonable and we could afford it so we all got our house built. We stayed involved in that co-op for about ten years, until we could get enough money to get a loan from a bank to buy ourselves out. We said thank God for Calvin Ruck. He started the East Preston Co-op. He was our saviour. This was the first Black co-op housing in the Preston area. We knew we wanted to build a house, but we didn't know how to get it."

"I can't drive through the community without looking at some of the houses that he helped facilitate the development of, the creation of. That was probably the next sort of life-changing thing for us," says Wanda Thomas Bernard.

Sitting in her beautifully renovated home in East Preston, Wanda tells the story of her mother's struggles with having a home of her own. "My mom was trying to build a house. The house we lived in could probably sit in these two rooms. It was a really tiny house and it was really rundown. It was really in poor condition. So she was talking with Calvin about building a house. The co-op movement was fabulous because they used the sweat equity. And she was working as a domestic. She didn't have a lot of money. But she was working and she was hard-working. And all she had to do was to have a clearer title to her land. And that's what she did not have. My father had never taken care of that, but we didn't know.

"I remember I was the person who went to the registry of deeds to get the deed. And to my surprise, the property belonged to my uncle. By this time, my grandfather was ill (my father's father) and we lived across from him. In those days that's how people did it. My dad's name was Jimmy and it was, 'Okay, Jimmy, you can have this place over here and build a house on it.' They built some sort of house and that was the end of it. Well, my father died, and my grandfather became ill and his youngest son moved in with his wife to look after him and he signed everything over to his youngest son. Including the property we lived on. So imagine our surprise when I go to the registry of deeds and try to get the deed and I find I can't get the deed because the property belongs to my uncle."

Wanda and her sister Valerie approached their uncle about their findings, but his solution was to allow them to stay on the property while charging them rent. "We had to go back across the road and tell Mom what happened. It's bad enough living in a shack, but if you've got to live in a shack and pay rent to your brother-in-law for it … There was no way my mom was having that. So that's why we moved to Dartmouth. And that's forty years ago. So we couldn't build the house because we couldn't get a clear title to the land. And I think Mr. Ruck was working with Mom trying to buy land someplace else [in the Preston community] but by then her heart wasn't in it."

The Land Titles Clarification Act proved to be one of the best learning experiences for many residents in the community, but for some, it came too late. "Because of Calvin, the land classification [clarification] was done and he got the Prestons to get their land titles cleared," says Dolly Williams. "People got upset when they first started talking about it thinking they [the government] were going to steal their land. Well, they're not going to steal your land. Once you get a clear title and a deed, the land will be yours. But right now, there's no clear titles. So Calvin came and had meetings with the community, explaining what was going on and how people are losing their properties all over, not just in our area. So Calvin got us onto the land clarification titles. He worked so hard for that. He worked with people more than once, especially older people, to make sure they understood, because a lot of people didn't read. He was so patient.

"My father, being stubborn, would not. Doug [Ruck] was our lawyer. So we went to do it when my father got sick, in the hospital, and Doug said to us, 'If you don't do it, the government's going to take the land.' But I said to Doug, 'If Daddy had done this years ago, we wouldn't be where we are now.' But in the meantime, we wouldn't have had land either because the government would have taken it back."

Prior to 1972, Preston residents could not take advantage of the Land Titles Clarification Act. An area could only benefit from the act if the government designated it as a land titles clarification area. Because many of these homes were passed down through generations, there were no clear titles or way of tracing back to a proper deed. Without this designation, no one held title to their home and the land was considered Crown land. Calvin viewed having the deed to one's home as a basic human right and he began to share the necessary steps of becoming a designated area with several people in the community.

"When he got involved with community services, he used to visit a lot of homes and find out what people needed," recalls Marilyn Smith. "I can remember him sitting here talking to Mom and my mother never liked handouts. And did they argue. There was no indoor plumbing until we took over the old home and that's what he was trying to get her to do."

For Calvin, this was not a handout. These were rights every human being deserved and if other communities had deeds to their homes, land titles and proper plumbing, then why wouldn't these Black communities have all of that and more?

"He just wasn't interested in the essentials like housing and jobs," says Valerie Ruck. "He was interested in their whole lives. He wanted to give them as many life experiences as possible."

"People were getting inside plumbing and there were a few televisions and everybody was getting the amenities and feeling really good about themselves," Carolyn says with a smile. "But I think that the title was one of the big things."

In 1972, East Preston and a part of North Preston were designated as a land titles clarifcation area, and individuals could then attempt to receive deeds and take proper ownership of their land.

"It was their property," adds Carolyn. "Their homes. That was a big thing. This land was Crown land. Granted land. It was like the forty acres and the mule. You were promised them, but you never really got them. You didn't really get the title to the land. You were like a squatter on your land because you didn't get the title. He helped to fight to effect that change [by using] the Land Clarifications Title Act. Like a lot of legislation, it was for everybody else, but it was not for us. He had that vision. He's saying, 'Well, if this instrument is here, then why is it not applicable here? If we got the mortgage companies and housing and what it says it stands for, why is it not applicable here?' People appreciated it.

"The long-term is very prevalent. People tend to forget because they don't talk about it. But once you stir it up, they're quick to remind you of who was instrumental in helping to bring about the change. It's long-term because now on a parcel of land there are houses where there was initially a house. So there's the multiplying effect. These houses and subdivisions stand as a testament to their work and in particular Mr. Ruck's effort."

Calvin's efforts were also focused on community buildings such as daycare facilities and medical centres. For other neighbourhoods these facilities would be considered the norm, but for North and East Preston, Lake Loon and Cherry Brook, such simple structures were nowhere to be found. Calvin wasn't the only one who noticed these essentials were missing in these communities. Dr. John Savage was saddened and shocked to see the lack of accessible medical facilities.

"My father was on duty one day and somebody had come in from the community of Preston," recounts Mike Savage. "He hadn't heard of it. And they didn't have a doctor; they had nothing. So he went out to do a

Calvin with John Savage (1932-2003), a family physician who became Mayor of Dartmouth (1985-1992) and Premier of Nova Scotia (1993-1997).

house call and he was kind of appalled at the condition of North Preston. So he started spending a lot of time there and they built a medical facility there and worked with others to put a childcare facility in. So he came across Calvin, along with other leaders and folks in the community. My dad and Calvin did a lot of work together on social activism causes."

Dr. Savage began spending more time in Preston and as a preceptor of family medicine, he decided to give his students some hands-on training in North Preston. "Today, medical students go all over the world," says Mike Savage. "They go to Rwanda, they go to Nigeria, they go to Thailand and they learn, but back in the day, medical students basically went to medical school so they could get their degree and come out and make a bit of money and raise their family. I think that taking them to North Preston in those days to a clinic was for two purposes. One was so that they would get a wider sense of what a medical career is about, but it also provided staff for the medical clinic in North Preston."

Calvin and Dr. Savage had a common goal for progress and social change. "With my father, if he saw a problem, he would throw everything at it to solve it and one of the things that holds people back from making social progress is that they're not confident enough in themselves to be the solution," says Mike Savage. "And what my father believed and I think what Calvin believed was that you go headlong into it and you bring people with you. You don't have to be the expert. Somebody can solve it. But somebody's got to get the ball rolling. So I suspect that both believed in that. They were both passionate about social justice issues and fundamentally believed in equality and as much as anything else, equality of opportunity. My father certainly stressed with us a lot that we were privileged. We were a large family. We weren't a rich family, but we were a pretty comfortable family and certainly one of the things that both my mother and father emphasized with us was the sense that those to whom much is given, much is expected. And I would expect that the same was expected of the Ruck family."

Dr. Savage also made a point of bringing his children to North Preston. "It was very unusual for Dartmouth kids, white kids, to go out to North Preston. We spent a lot of time there and got to know a lot of the kids up there. I think my father wanted that. He wanted us to understand that so it wasn't this much of a big deal."

These new developments also meant labour jobs were opening up and Calvin made sure local men were being chosen to carry out these tasks. "He was the employment officer; he made work for the community," says Gary Johnson. "He developed trade through housing development. He made sure that they hired men from the area and he made sure that the men were given training."

These men were not master carpenters, and for some, their experience and education in the trade was quite limited. But that didn't stop Calvin from motivating them to try. Proper training was at the top of his priority list and if the men were willing to learn, then he was willing to resource the right people and tools to teach them.

"He showed them the proper way of doing it and how to do it so you won't be breaking the law and how to build by code. When you buy building supply it's all done by code. He showed them how that is done. And he helped the handymen to be better educated and be better handymen and carpenters. They weren't the kind of carpenters that they should have been so he created education for them. Some of them still call themselves carpenters," Gary says with a laugh.

Calvin would invite anyone who was interested to his home to watch slide shows instructing beginners on how to build a home. He used a projector and a white sheet to display the images, and men and women came to the Ruck home to educate themselves on the trade.

As someone who was involved in so much and vocal about many issues, Calvin's name became very familiar to the people of Nova Scotia. The phrase "You can't please everyone" was a daily reminder in Calvin's life. For every person who was grateful for the changes, there was someone else who was looking for the first opportunity to shut down this man who seemed to have no fear. The family was never really worried about his safety until he appeared on a local television show. It all began when his eldest son, Doug, went to a local barbershop to get his hair cut on his school lunch break in 1964.

"Before the barbershop opened on Main Street, someone had canvassed the neighbourhoods to see if the area would support the business. I believe that someone had come to our place on Walker Street and we indicated support for the idea."

Bringing along two friends, fourteen-year-old Doug was just looking for a quick haircut and then would head back to school. It seemed routine enough for Doug, but he quickly found out the barber had a very specific clientele.

"He took me aside and said, 'I don't cut coloured people's hair.'

"I was completely oblivious to the possibility that I might be refused service. I was completely shocked when the barber drew me aside, after I indicated that I was the one there for the haircut, and told me he would not cut my hair. I think I may have mumbled something about telling my father and then going back to my friends and telling them we were leaving. On the way back to school I explained to them what had happened. They were shocked and I think remained silent most of the way back. I was embarrassed, hurt, and close to tears. I thought the afternoon would never end as all I wanted was to go home and tell Dad what had happened."

After school that day, Doug explained to his father why he had not gotten a haircut. That same day, Calvin went back to that same barbershop. This time he took his youngest son, Martin. Calvin believed his son, but he had to hear it for himself if he was going to do something about it. Although it happened when he was just five years old, Martin still remembers walking into that small barbershop on Main Street with his father.

"When Dad took me to get a haircut, I knew something was up because he always cut my hair and had never taken me to a barbershop before. There was a man getting a haircut and two barbers: one cutting hair and the other one was reading the paper. They wanted to know what we wanted and Dad said he would like to get his son's hair cut. The one barber cutting the man's hair indicated that there was no one there to do that. And the other barber reading the paper didn't speak. I remember Dad asking him if he spoke and whether he would cut my hair and I recall he didn't say anything. Just shook his head that he wouldn't cut my hair. I also remember Dad asking the man who was getting his hair cut if he would serve as witness and he said yes.

"What I remember the most is that Dad didn't get mad. He was very calm and polite. He was very friendly and respectful to them – which in retrospect perhaps made it all the more surreal. Then Dad took me back to the car and told me to 'wait here and don't touch anything.' And then he went back in with a pad of paper. It seemed like he was in there for a long time and I remember being aware of what was going on and feeling funny because I was happy that I wasn't going to have to get my hair cut. I knew that it was a serious matter but didn't realize the enormity of it.

"Then Dad came back to the car and we drove to a couple of other barbershops, finally finding one that would cut my hair. I think it was one by the old Capitol store. Then several days later I remember it being on the news that a local man was using the recent Nova Scotia Human Rights Act [passed in 1963] to challenge barbershops that discriminated on race and ethnicity. As they put it, 'refused to cut negroes' hair.' The news story also said that Mr. Ruck would be returning to the barbershop with his son until they cut his hair."

"I remember the kids were outside and I said, 'Come in. Your father's going to be on television,'" recalls Joyce. "And the people who lived next door heard me because they all ran in the house too. He was always on television."

The news brought mixed emotions in the Ruck household as Joyce was more concerned with her son's safety than anything else. She was not pleased that Martin had been mentioned in the story. "She had Dad call the TV station to make sure that they didn't mention me in the future. I think she didn't want people thinking that they would use their son for any type of political gain."

Joyce admits that although she may have been opposed to some of the things Calvin was doing out of fear for his safety, she rarely spoke up about it.

"Even if I was opposed, I don't know if I ever told him. I might have said, 'Calvin, I don't think you should do that,' but he would go ahead and do it anyways because he felt it had to be done, like getting your hair cut."

In the Dartmouth *Free Press*, a local newspaper, Edmund Morris stated, "This barber should drown in his own spittoon." Calvin was no longer fighting his battles alone. He had the attention of the media, and the support of a few, but a face was now associated with the name, and although good exposure for a noble cause, it also meant people would be able to recognize who Calvin was and make their decisions about him before he even opened his mouth.

"In those days, racism was so in your face and he was one of those people that would not tolerate that," says Caroyln Thomas. "He was a man of dignity and respect and by his mere presence, he demanded the same. He was a firm man. You don't mess with this man. I think it made me want to become a little bit of a rebel."

The more vocal he became, the more adversaries he gained, and while it was his name being linked to these issues, his family was beginning to feel the effects. Hate mail and anonymous phone calls continued and some late nights were in store for the Ruck family. Calvin was now being labelled as a "troublemaker" and some went so far as to suggest he was associated with the Black radical group, the Black Panthers. "Calvin said to me, 'Well, I guess I'll be a troublemaker if I have to fight for what's right," recalls Joyce. "He said, 'I don't want my children going through what I went through.'"

"I had great fear for Dad every time he was out in the evening attending meetings," remembers Doug. "Mom was even more nervous than I was and would never go to bed until Dad came home. I spent a great many evenings sitting up with her and looking out the window to spot the car coming up the street. It was always an extraordinary sense of relief when the car would pull into the driveway."

Calvin's constant workload impacted his entire family, but there was a silent understanding that these things had to be done and they would see him when the work was finished. "We came to accept it as part of our lifestyle," says Doug.

While Calvin had social activism and community development on the mind, for a young boy who just came along for the ride, Doug had other worries at the time. "If Dad pulled into certain yards, I said, 'Oh, no, I'm going to be late for the dance tonight.'" And while he was thinking it, you can be sure he was not planning on expressing this any time soon to his father. "I never said anything to him," Doug laughs. "I knew his thoughts were, 'No dance is that important. I'm out here earning a living and how do you think you got money to go to the dance?' Now if I had to go to a meeting to discuss human rights, then that would be important. But I really enjoyed being with him on Saturdays. I knew he was taking his time to discuss important issues. I knew the reality of it."

While other children were relaxing or playing with their friends on the weekend, Doug's time with his father on those Saturdays gave him a strong bond with Calvin, and through watching his father, the young boy learned the value of integrity.

6: WE SERVE

IN JUNE OF 1977, JAMES E. Brindley formed and chartered the East Preston Lions Club.

"Jim was sort of the father of the Lions, because people had approached him about a service club for the area and he had talked to men in the community about the possibilities and they looked at different models to see what would be best," explains Carolyn Thomas. "They decided the Lions would be because it was more like us. It was more open; not as business oriented, more social oriented. Then they were talking about organizing the women's arm. They said get Carolyn. She'll organize. I said, 'I can't do that.' And they cornered me!"

The service organization, which set out to meet the needs of the community through fundraising, public awareness and the simple act of helping the common man became a staple in the community. Your fellow Lions and Lionesses were your family and when a Lion was in need, you can be sure there were several men and women with their gold and blue baseball hats and vests ready and willing to help.

"The Lions Club is work and play," says Carolyn "The motto, which Mr. Ruck and the Lions sang, is, 'We serve.' It's service all the way. When the women came alongside with the Lioness, the motto internationally was, 'We serve too.'"

Calvin was constantly finding activities for the Lions to be a part of, from locating housing to the simplest act of planting flowers. "He included the Lions program for World Service Day," says Carolyn. "We had to do an activity in the community, but it had to include the church. That's how the flower garden started in front of our church – as a world service project. And it does not look the same since Mr. Ruck was doing it. He just went and got all the flowers and was out there even at night. If there were any left over, I think he would give them to some of the seniors."

Although the organization is not as prominent in the East Preston area as it was a decade or two ago, the pride and respect of the veteran Lion men and women is still strong. This was most apparent when chatting with Carolyn in her home. As she reminisced about times gone by, her husband Matthew appeared around the corner. I was immediately taken back to the days when Calvin was preparing to attend a Lions' meeting.

Matthew approached wearing black dress pants and a crisp white shirt under the Lions' signature vest, with necktie in hand. Calvin would have been proud. "When somebody mentions Calvin Ruck, you've got to get dressed up for the occasion," Matthew says with a smile.

Matthew and Calvin spent a lot of time together, setting up scholarships, selling chocolate bars at the local malls for fundraisers, and as Matthew puts it, they were "digging into everything."

"He really took the bull by the horns. Calvin Ruck dug his heels in and made sure things took place. It was a real challenge. He wanted to see things nicely laid out. When he wasn't down in Westphal working on the house, he was out here in Preston. I can see him now."

"And if a Lion died, then they were part of the memorial tributes," adds Carolyn. "To this day, even on Remembrance Day when the Girl Guides, etc. do a special service, the Lions were included to make a special presentation. Back then, and to this day. It's all of these things that came as a result of Mr. Ruck."

While Calvin was busy in the community encouraging others to further themselves and broaden their knowledge, he was also actively living out those words in his own life. If there was a learning opportunity, Calvin was absolutely going to take advantage of it. "He saw society becoming more and more complex," says Doug. "Even though he was working all the time, he somehow found a way to fit these courses in. Some would be a week and some would be months."

In 1978, Calvin decided to enroll in the Maritime School of Social Work at Dalhousie University. "I remember that," says Carolyn. "That was a big thing in the community, from a pride perspective. It was an encouragement. If he could do it, I could do it."

Calvin was working as a community development officer at the time and worked alongside many who had earned a degree in the field of social work. Although doing many of the duties a social worker would do, he was not earning the same pay, so Calvin went back to school. "He was working as a community development officer, but he knew he wanted to do more," adds Wanda Thomas Bernard. "And he knew he could do more."

Calvin spent many late nights studying and, as Joyce recalls, he enjoyed every minute of it. "We'd be gone to bed and Calvin would be up studying, but he enjoyed it. He was the oldest person there, but he enjoyed the young people."

Around that time, Valerie was dating Doug. Aspiring to be a teacher, Valerie would help Calvin with his statistics studies. She also has never forgotten how full the Ruck pantry was of canned food. "Joyce had a pantry cupboard filled with canned food because he was going full-time to the Maritime School of Social Work so he wouldn't be getting full salary."

During her life with Calvin, Joyce had developed a number of money-saving strategies. Economizing wherever she could was one way of supporting Calvin in his endeavours. "I was very thrifty," says Joyce. "Calvin gave me all of the money and I was in charge of how it was spent." Calvin's long hours and Joyce's money management proved to be effective, as lack of money was never a conversation in the Ruck household. Doug notes that it never occurred to him his family may have been considered poor.

"We didn't know as kids that we were poor. We honestly thought we were middle-class, particularly because most of the neighbourhood was in that same state."

While Calvin was in his first year at Dalhousie, the East Preston Centennial Centre held a night of recognition for his work in youth education, housing and recreation.

As opposed to the many articles published about the backlash Calvin was getting for his efforts, Halifax's *The Mail Star* had this to say of the evening: "In acting as the community social worker and social development officer for the Preston area for the past ten years, Mr. Ruck has earned the respect and admiration not only of the community residents, but also of Nova Scotians of all creeds and colours." The article went on to list Calvin's many involvements: "Mr. Ruck ... is a member of the Nova Scotia Association for the Advancement of Coloured People, a commissioner of the Supreme Court of Nova Scotia, an ex-officio board member of the Preston Area Housing Fund, a member of the North Preston Child Care Society, East Preston's Lions Club, and East Preston Recreation Association, and finds time to serve as a deacon of Stevens Road United Baptist Church."

Calvin enjoyed every minute of his time at the school and became quite popular among staff and peers of the Maritime School of Social Work. "He was well-known. It's pretty hard not to know Calvin," says Joan Gilroy, a former director of the school. "I think people liked him, loved him, trusted him, felt his interest in them and they were interested in him. I think it was his wonderful being."

In 1979, at fifty-four years of age, Calvin graduated. "He really was a social worker all his life when you think of it," says Joyce.

Doug had opened his own law practice by that time and says watching his father not only walk across the stage and receive his diploma, but also be awarded for the highest mark in the course was "almost surreal. It was amazing to see my father, who was such a strong believer in education, attain a goal that he himself, at times, had thought was not possible. Not only was I proud of Dad, but he was so well respected and liked that the entire student body cheered for him. What was even more astounding was the fact he had thought he would fail statistics as he simply could not grasp the various concepts. He worked very hard on that course."

Joyce and Calvin in 1994 when he was awarded an honourary degree from Dalhousie University.

"I think he had quite a positive influence at the school," adds Wanda Thomas Bernard. "Some of the faculty members that taught him still talk about him."

Wanda continues to be a part of a group called the Minorities Task Force at the School of Social Work. "Once they began a standing committee they had decision-making power. It was quite a significant move from a task force to a standing committee. They had a Name the Committee contest and Calvin came up with the name COREA [Committee on Racial and Ethnic Affairs]. And that name stood until quite recently. We only changed it in recent years because we started to expand the equity issues so the committee is now the Diversity and Equity Committee. I've served as director for ten years and Calvin's influence there has been very positive."

His influence includes a Dr. Calvin W. Ruck Scholarship, established in 1998, given annually to "African Nova Scotian students in the Master of Social Work or Bachelor of Social Work programs at the School of Social Work, who demonstrate a desire to improve and advance the interests of African Nova Scotian and African Canadian people through the study and practice of social work."

As Joan explains, the scholarship was established by the Nova Scotia Association for the Advancement of Coloured People (NSAACP), who decided to split their funds towards three different focuses of study. "After many years of very devoted work on the part of Calvin and many others, they were getting older and the younger people were coming in to take up the work of the society. So they felt that they had done the best they could and now they would fold up and hope that other groups would take up the struggle. They had some money left and they took a fairly long time deciding what they were going to do with it and education being a very strong theme for Calvin and others, he wanted a portion to go to the school and a portion to go to the law school, because Gus Wedderburn [who went to the law school as a mature student] was still living. The third portion went to the [James R.] Johnston Chair in Black Canadian Studies, which they were just organizing at that time. So they divided the funds fairly among the three places. The idea was education and to carry forward the struggle against racism in the world."

"The award is given to a social work student who really tries to uphold the values and principles that Calvin upheld," says Wanda, adding that her daughter has been granted the award twice to aid in her schooling.

"He was a special type of person," says Joan. "We were lucky. He came to our field. Because he could have done so many things."

Dalhousie hosted a reception when the NSAACP gave the funds to the university. With Calvin and Gus in attendance, Joan says it made for a very memorable gathering.

"Calvin and Gus told us so many of the stories and it was just a wonderful reception. You know how usually you stand around and have a glass in your hand and chat with people you don't know. It was just really an educational experience that was fun and warm. I had organized it so

I was delighted that it went so well. I know if Calvin was there, it was going to be a happy occasion."

In 1981, while Calvin was working in the Family Benefits Division of the provincial Department of Social Services, he was appointed to the Nova Scotia Human Rights Commission as a human rights officer. Carolyn Thomas was also working at the commission at the time, under the direction of Dr. George McCurdy.

"I was in a supervisor position and I remember Mr. Ruck applying and I remember saying, 'Oh wow, Mr. Ruck! Yeah, we need him!' And I remember talking to Dr. McCurdy and saying, 'We need that man in here.' And I kept saying, 'I'm going to be a supervisor to Mr. Ruck? Come on, give me a break!'"

Although she occupied a higher position, Carolyn's respect and admiration for Calvin were great and she made sure everyone else showed him that same respect. "I remember one day, we were working together and the chief human rights officer called for Mr. Ruck and said, 'Calvin, can I see you?' And I said, 'Calvin? What's he talking about?' And I went into his office when they got finished and I was almost in tears and I said to him, 'You must never call him Calvin; that is Mr. Ruck.' I think from that day, he was Mr. Ruck. I don't care if he was the junior officer coming in here or whatever, he is not Calvin; he is Mr. Ruck."

Throughout his work in community development and human rights, Calvin took many of his cues from the Civil Rights Movements in the U.S., referencing Martin Luther King, Jr. as an inspiration for his work in human rights. Calvin's style of fighting for justice and equality could also be attributed to King. Although admitting he struggled with anger constantly, King always looked at the bigger picture and reminded himself not to mimic the emotions of his opponents. In his autobiography, King wrote:

> *I was weighed down by a terrible sense of guilt, remembering that on two or three occasions I had allowed myself to become angry and indignant. I had spoken hastily and resentfully. Yet I knew that this was no way to solve a problem. 'You must not harbor anger,' I admonished myself. 'You must be willing to suffer the anger of the opponent, and yet not return anger. You*

must not become bitter. No matter how emotional your opponents are, you must be calm.

Calvin's ability to stir the pot while calming the waters was a unique gift and it did not go unnoticed. "He was very sensitive, approachable, respectful, but also very committed and dedicated," recalls Wanda. "If he was focused on an issue, you weren't going to persuade him to leave it alone if he didn't win. He was going to stay with it, but not in an aggressive way, in a very assertive way. If people don't see you as aggressive, they think you're passive, but what they don't know is there's a thing called assertiveness. If you're fighting for a situation or for a cause, what do you want people to remember? Do you want them to remember that you were in there fighting or do you want them to remember what you were fighting for? Calvin Ruck was the type of person, when he left a situation, you knew what he was fighting for and you knew what he stood for. You don't remember that he was fighting because he didn't fight in a way that seemed like a fight. It was a perspective that he was presenting. He could present a perspective in a way that you stopped and you listened. When he spoke, you wanted to listen."

As Joyce watched her husband deal with the day-in and day-out battles of racism and human rights, she asked him how he managed to stay calm throughout. "I always used to ask Calvin, 'Why don't you get angry?' and he would say, 'Joyce, there's too much to be done. I don't have time to be angry.'" The time that could have been spent harbouring anger and resentment was instead used to effect change.

While Calvin spent a good majority of his time working in these Black communities, there was one area of his life that was completely separate from this work. Calvin and Joyce were active members of Stevens Road United Baptist Church. Calvin was determined to be seen as part of the Westphal community and being a member of that community included going to a church that was just a few blocks away.

"He was living in a white community, and he said he thought he should live where he wanted to live and I agree with this," says Joan Gilroy. "Even though it must have been terrible, he persisted. He wanted to go to the church he wanted to go to. I think he got some criticism for not going to a so-called Black church. That was very unusual too.

He was a very strong member of the church. He was oriented to the neighbourhood and this was his neighbourhood church."

For Calvin and Joyce this just made sense and they were happy there, making lifelong friends with many of its attendants. But to others, a Black man attending a predominantly white church, especially when there were predominantly Black churches in Preston, was unheard of and perhaps a little insulting to some. "We had people representing the Black church," says Dr. Pachai. "He was the only one who didn't represent the church and he was therefore not shackled by the church. Calvin always took an open mind."

Just like every other area of his life, Calvin chose not to be a spectator and became actively involved in church duties. "For him, to just go to a church and sit there on a Sunday morning wasn't really attending a church," says Jacqueline. "Community was very important to him. So to Granddad, it was important to become a deacon; it was important to him to become involved in any way that he could because he did not believe in just taking. He believed in giving."

Among other roles, he was on the deacon board and was head of security, while Joyce sang in the choir. Always looking to progress and move forward, Calvin introduced the church's first security system. "They didn't have any security before that," says Valerie, who also attended Stevens Road. "They thought, 'We're just a little church. Why would we need security?' But he thought it doesn't matter what size the church is, you should have the same rules in place and the same things that bigger churches would also have. He was good at making people gain confidence."

Calvin attended member meetings and church picnics. His faith was strong, and those Sunday mornings were a time for him to be refreshed and rejuvenated and to spend quality time with his biological and church family.

"He would start all of his speeches that I can remember with, 'To God be the glory, great things he has done,'" recalls Jacqueline. "I remember sitting in crowds filled with dignitaries and hearing him recite a Bible verse and thinking that probably takes courage because it's not necessarily the popular thing to be a Christian in this day and age, and yet he was very unapologetic about it and regardless of who he was speaking to and what important person was in the room, it didn't matter. He was going to start a speech giving all glory to God."

"It didn't matter where he was," adds Valerie. "Whether it was a large auditorium at Dalhousie University or a small church, he always said, 'To God be the glory.'"

It is no surprise then that in the acknowledgements in Calvin's first book he gave a "heartfelt thanks to our Lord and Saviour for his gifts of love, health, strength, interest and desire, which enabled me to persevere."

Calvin spent a great deal of time uncovering what he called "Canada's best kept military secret." And while he was working to change the futures of Blacks in Nova Scotia, he was also preparing to unveil the past of the No. 2 Black Construction Battalion, Canadian Expeditionary Force (C.E.F.).

7: Canada's Best Kept Military Secret

On July 6, 2013, at the twentieth commemoration of the No. 2 Construction Battalion in Pictou, Nova Scotia, the local town crier, George Dooley, gives the official proclamation, addressing the crowd to kick off the ceremony. Reading from a scroll in a booming voice, he recounts being called upon by an "energetic man" twenty years ago to be a part of the first commemorative ceremony. He goes on to explain that this man was Calvin W. Ruck. The crowd nods, and smiles cross their faces as they had no doubt of whom George Dooley was speaking. It is apparent that everyone, many who have faithfully attended this event for twenty years, is there because of one man's determination to bring this story into the light and recognize these soldiers as best as he could.

The No. 2 Construction Battalion was authorized in 1916, under the command of Lieutenant-Colonel D.H. Sutherland of River John, Pictou County, Nova Scotia. Its creation was the Canadian Armed Forces' solution to the many Black volunteers who were being turned away when trying to enlist to serve their country in the First World War. Many were simply told, "This is a white man's war." While enlistment for this segregated battalion was carried out across Canada, Nova Scotia provided the largest single group, recording approximately three hundred men volunteering for service in what came to be called The Black Battalion.

Calvin was unable to serve in the Second World War because of problems with his eyes and his feet. But as a historian and a scholar, he was always fascinated with the subject. His educational journey with the No. 2 Construction Battalion began when he was working as a sleeping car porter. Older Black gentlemen would come on the train wearing a small pin. Upon inquiry, Calvin was told it represented the No. 2 Construction Battalion. This was the first he had heard of the battalion and it immediately sparked his interest and curiosity.

The all-Black construction unit was designated to support the front lines by building roads and bridges, defusing land mines to allow the advancing troops to move forward, and retrieving the wounded.

"I remember being quite young and Dad telling me these little snippets about the No. 2 Construction Battalion – which I had no interest in whatsoever," Doug recalls. "As a five- or seven-year-old, that wasn't what you wanted to hear. As he went on, he became determined and I got more interested in it as well and he started doing the research and you realized it really was almost a secret."

Calvin's research was extensive as he contacted family members, historians, the National Archives and anyone who may have had any nugget of information on this little-known but great historical group. "My father's never written a book before and that was immaterial," says Doug. "You simply just sat down and started writing. That was it. And then he started calling people." Calvin unearthed documents that were most likely seen by few and their existence unknown to most.

"No one really knew about it, in my opinion," says Wayne Adams. "My generation was saying, 'You've got to be kidding. Is this a fairytale?' He did all that research, he got all those photos. He was linking families together and people were saying, 'No one ever told me that.' That's the mark of the man. That was a major move in his career."

Of particular interest to Calvin was a diary written by the Reverend Captain William A. White, chaplain of the No. 2 Construction Battalion and, reportedly, the only Black commissioned officer in the British Armed Forces during World War I. White was a native of Williamsburg, Virginia, and came to Nova Scotia in 1899. In 1919, following service overseas, White came to Halifax and became pastor of the Cornwallis Street Baptist Church. Reverend White's daughter, the late Portia White, was a gifted operatic contralto who went on to be the first Black Canadian concert singer to reach international fame. In May of 1936, Reverend White received a doctorate of divinity from his alma mater, Acadia University, making him the first Black Canadian to be given an honourary degree.

In his research, Calvin discovered harsh words that painted a pitiful and inaccurate picture of the Black man. In April of 1916, in a memorandum on the enlistment of negroes in Canadian Expeditionary Force, Sir Willoughby Garnons Gwatkin, KCMG, CB, the Chief of the General Staff, had this to say about Blacks fighting side by side with white soldiers:

> *Nothing is to be gained by blinking facts. The civilized negro is vain and imitative; in Canada he is not being impelled to enlist by a high sense of duty; in the trenches he is not likely to make a good fighter; and the average white man will not associate with him on terms of equality. Not a single commanding officer in Military District No. 2 is willing to accept a coloured platoon as part of his battalion (H.Q. 297-1-29); and it would be humiliating to the coloured men themselves to serve in a battalion where they were not wanted.*

Calvin knew a thing or two about not being wanted and had heard ridiculous reason upon reason about why he just didn't fit in.

"Nobody was writing about it or had written about it with that same amount of depth," says Bridglal Pachai. "He was working with the Black community and he was talking to relatives of the soldiers who enlisted. In fact, he spoke to many of them on a personal level. He knew them on a marvelous level. He was the first man to do that."

Although he gives only a brief mention of the battalion in *The Blacks in Canada: A History*, historian Robin Winks penned one of the few published works that noted the No. 2.

"While in military history, the name was there, the founding was there, but the personalities who were involved in it from the Black community were never recorded until Calvin's book appeared," says Dr. Pachai. "That's the marvelous feature of that book, because a book must give life to its characters. Not in the captions only. Not in the laws that were passed. Not in the regulations that were made. Their lives would be recorded to make it meaningful, to give the title its strength and its permanence and Calvin did that. He was the first man to do that. It was not that it was not known, but it was known without its flesh."

As Calvin was putting together his first drafts, he was also sharing his findings with his colleagues. Joan Gilroy, who upon Calvin's request read these early drafts of the book, says it was the first she had heard of the topic and was captivated.

"Calvin was very open and he wanted me to know about it," she recounts. "I found it fascinating. He knew so much about it and he had researched it thoroughly."

Calvin dedicated the book to the "memory of all Blacks who served in the Great War, 1914-1918." In the preface, Calvin explained why he was determined to write this book:

> The Black military heritage in Canada is still generally unknown and unwritten. Many Canadians of all races have no idea that Blacks served, fought, bled and died on European battlefields, all in the name of freedom. That fact that approximately six hundred Black soldiers served in a segregated non-combatant labour battalion during World War I had been one of the best kept secrets in Canadian military history.
>
> The story of the overt racist treatment of Black volunteers is a shameful chapter in the history of this country. It does, however, represent an important part of the Black legacy and the Black experience.
>
> Lest we forget.

"At that time, Canada was becoming more of a nation that was concerned about all its parts – trying to become more and more inclusive," says Dr. Pachai. "He was there on the front line, in the civilian front line when the word 'inclusive' was there in the English dictionary but it was not there in societal practice. So his book was an example of bringing forward inclusiveness and putting the Black partners in the forefront. That's what that book represents."

Prior to the release of the book, Calvin, along with Bridglal Pachai, Henry Bishop, Carolyn Thomas, Wayne Adams and other members of the Black Cultural Centre, planned a tribute evening to those Black soldiers who were still living. The evening would later be recorded in the pages of Calvin's book, calling it "a night to remember."

"We had a lot of volunteers involved," says Wayne. "Calvin was a respected voice throughout the province so when he called people in the communities to do something, they by and large did it."

Locating and organizing men from all over the country was not an easy task, but the sight of proud Black veterans who were finally getting the long overdue respect and dignity they so deserved made the long hours and hard work all worth it.

"It was at the Lord Nelson Hotel," recalls Carolyn. "He [Calvin] would tell them, 'We need this ballroom and we need this.' To see those veterans that night – I can remember going up on the landing and looking down and seeing them in wheelchairs. Seeing these people come and converge upon the ballroom at the Lord Nelson Hotel – that was a significant thing in itself. But they came together. It was a big thing."

The Reunion and Recognition Banquet was held November 12, 1982, and was attended by nine of the approximately twenty known surviving Black veterans. William Carter (No. 2), John W. Hamilton (No. 2), Percy J. Richards (No. 2), Gordon C. Wilson (No. 2), Albert D. Deleon (Canadian Forestry Corps), A. Seymour Tyler (No. 2), Sydney M. Jones (106BN, The Royal Canadian Regiment), Isaac Phills (85BN), and John R. Pannill (Merchant Navy) were reunited and honoured not only for their bravery during wartime, but for representing a small group of soldiers who made great strides for respect and equality.

"It was timely because a lot of the veterans have now passed on and if he hadn't have done it when he did, they wouldn't have had that number of veterans show up," says Wayne. "That was a comment by a lot of people, saying, 'Man, what timing!' It had to be divinely driven. They had to live for that event to take place."

"These are unsung heroes of our society," adds Henry. "We always look for the bigger than life heroes sometimes and get caught

Veterans of the First World War attend the Reunion and Recognition Banquet at the Lord Nelson Hotel, November 12, 1982. Front row, left to right: William Carter, John W. Hamilton, Percy J. Richards, Gordon C. Wilson, Albert D. Deleon. Second row, left to right: A. Seymour Tyler, Sydney M. Jones, Isaac Phills, John R. Pannill.

up in the celebrity status, whereas this book gave me and others a common denominator. Everybody was feeling, that's my uncle, that's my grandfather, that's my cousin. Someway there was a connector that made them feel good about themselves because this individual served his country so well."

The Halifax *Mail Star* reported, "The Imperial Ballroom at the Lord Nelson Hotel was packed last night with nearly 300 guests for the first and perhaps only reunion of Black First World War Veterans."

Canada's Black Battalion, No. 2 Construction C.E.F., was originally published in 1986 by The Society for the Protection and Preservation of Black Culture in Nova Scotia (The Black Cultural Centre) and then reprinted by Nimbus Publishing of Halifax in 1987. Henry Bishop says he will never forget that moment. "This history was worthy of being written down," he says. "Documentation means that it's in black and white. It stands the test of time and has validation and importance. It connects people of today to people of yesterday. It made people take notice. It created momentum. That was a life-stirring element of my existence here. Seeing how these people suffered so much. The indignities. They didn't talk about them until the book came out."

Bridglal Pachai, who was the director of the Centre at that time, recalls planning the book launch in 1986. "When the first edition appeared, I was then the head of the Black Cultural Society," he says. "When we launched the book, I called Robert Stanfield to do the launching. [Stanfield, 1914-2003, was premier of Nova Scotia from 1956 to 1967, then leader of the national Progressive Conservative Party from 1967 to 1976.] Robert Stanfield was a gentleman of the highest order. It was he who through his philosophy did a lot for the Black community. And he was going to London, but he said to me, I will be there at the book launch. He went to London, returned to Ottawa, took a flight, almost the next connection to Halifax, and came to launch the book. Robert Stanfield understood the early years of the No. 2 Construction Battalion, that the headquarters were in Pictou, but the second one was in Truro and that was Stanfield's base."

The launch proved to be a success and the reception the book received was overwhelming. "There was a lot of anticipation for the book," says Wayne. "It's been highlighted for years ever since in different venues." People were talking, some for the first time, about the No. 2. The conversation was so great that a second edition came out shortly after.

"It was a marvelous reception," recalls Dr. Pachai. "It became published afterwards. The first was the Black Cultural Centre with all its modesty and limited funds, it produced a book, but it didn't have the capacity that there is in the publishing world to distribute and publicize on a broader canvas. Then Nimbus [Publishing] took it over. The fact that Nimbus took it over and brought out another edition of the same book is a testimony of the reception that book got. There was a tremendous turnout at the Black Cultural Centre. Henry [Bishop] was involved with me in the organization of that event. We had the who's who of Nova Scotia and the metro area in particular at that function. White and Black. He [Calvin] always had a beautiful, clean record in Nova Scotia; the book enhanced it. Everything that he did enhanced his reputation. He didn't have to go out as a salesman to make a name for himself. His name was already part of the currency of personalities of Nova Scotia."

The Black Battalion 1916-1920: Canada's Best Kept Military Secret had increased the awareness of Black military service for many people throughout the nation, including Henry Bishop, who discovered a personal connection to this story. "My mother had uncles in the battalion and so I was like, 'What? I've never heard about this group,' and yet I had family in it. Dr. Ruck gave me all the insights into this history and I thought, 'Wow, how come I don't know this stuff myself? I don't know my own family.' So it was really an eye-opener for me. And he gave me the inspiration to follow through on more things, and one of the things that really sparked my interest is that my Uncle Benson, Arthur Benson Cromwell, when he passed away overseas, Senator Ruck asked me about his attestation papers and where his body was. Because after all that time, after his death, in 1917, no one knew what happened to him. Senator Ruck said, 'You have to check with the National Archives and with the War Museum in Ottawa,' and I was given the directions of where to go."

Inspired by Calvin, Henry was determined to find out more. "I found out that his body was in Juno, France – just a number, no name – and I got the information for that and gave it to my mother and she was just overwhelmed. She cried because nobody knew what had happened to Uncle Benson's body and it gave some closure to her. A big gap was there and he filled the gap. Dr. Ruck made the joints come together that were separated. It's kind of like broken hearts and he healed them."

Henry wasn't the only one inspired by Calvin's findings. Anthony Sherwood, long-time family friend, actor, director and film producer, also had a family connection to the battalion. Reverend William White was Anthony's great-uncle. In 2001, Anthony wrote, produced and starred in *Honour Before Glory*, a docudrama that centred around direct excerpts from White's diary.

While the book was the initial catalyst, Calvin and the Black Cultural Centre were determined to do more to honour these men. In October 1987, the Centre, Calvin, and the Town of Pictou began working together to acquire national recognition for the No. 2. Four years later, in August of 1991, the Town of Pictou officially declared the Market Wharf a local historic property because of its association with Canada's first and only Black Battalion. In 1992, the Historic Sites and Monuments Boards of Canada, after receiving a documented submission from the Black Battalion Memorial Committee, recommended to the federal government that the Market Wharf be designated as a National Historic Site. The government accepted this recommendation on December 11, 1992. Calvin had many talks with the mayor of Pictou, Lawrence LeBlanc, discussing the idea of an annual ceremony to commemorate the No. 2.

Lawrence LeBlanc, who spoke briefly at the twentieth anniversary commemoration ceremony, praising Calvin as a "gentleman of the highest regard," was completely cooperative when it came to arranging the ceremony in Pictou and was adamant that each year, the Town of Pictou would hold a ceremony to honour the Black Battalion. On a hot summer day, July 10, 1993, the first commemoration ceremony of the No. 2 Black Construction Battalion, along with the unveiling of a memorial monument, took place in Pictou. "If we could put that monument there, no matter how racist people are, if they could see the monument every day, downtown, by the waterfront, it would start to help the healing process," says Henry.

Planning this event was no small task, and Calvin pulled out all the stops to ensure this day would be memorable and would properly honour those who had served their country. Unfamiliar with the words "can't" or "impossible," Calvin began contacting dignitaries and public figures, and no name was too big to be out of reach.

"He said, 'I think we should get Colin Powell,'" recalls Henry. "And I was thinking, 'How are we going to get him?' 'I think we should write. I think we should try.' And we actually got a response and I couldn't believe it and the only reason he didn't come is because of the Gulf War. He wrote back saying he wanted to come. That's amazing."

While the American four-star general, who went on to become Chairman of the U.S. Joint Chiefs of Staff and the U.S. Secretary of State, was unable to attend, Calvin did manage to bring in a few heroes of the skies. "We had the Tuskegee Airmen [the first Black pilots and crewmen in the U.S. military who fought in World War II] come up and they drove all the way up from Florida in a convertible," says Henry. "The guy was like eighty years old and he said, 'I got this letter from this Senator Ruck

Calvin received an honourary degree from Dalhousie University in 1994. The University of King's College also presented him with an honourary doctorate of civil law in 1999.

guy inviting us to come up here.' We had people from those kinds of levels take an interest."

"There was nothing he didn't think he could accomplish," says Doug. "If they said no, he would find another way to go about it. So he created that in ourselves as children – you had to try."

"He wasn't afraid to ask anybody for anything if it would better people," says Valerie. "He asked the Prime Minister to give money for the commemoration in Pictou. He wasn't intimidated by rank. He realized that people were just people. I imagine he did ask things that didn't get granted, but that wouldn't bother him. He wouldn't get angry; he would just try another angle. He didn't accept defeat."

The nostalgia of that first ceremony is unforgettable, as hundreds gathered to honour the now not-so-secret No. 2 Black Construction Battalion. "When I went to Pictou that first time, it was a very moving experience," recalls Joan Gilroy. "I found it very moving. When I came home, I sat down at my computer and wrote a nomination form for his honourary degree at Dal."

While nominations are confidential, upon receiving word of the honour, Calvin immediately knew who to call. "I didn't say anything to him or to anyone really, except I told whoever was the director [of the School of Social Work] then and it was submitted to an honourary degree selection committee," explains Joan. "When he got word of it from the president at that time, he called me right away because he knew. He said, 'You did this, didn't you?' And I didn't know what to say. I didn't want to lie to him, but I was also very familiar with the university's policy on confidentiality. I sort of had to tell him."

In front of Dalhousie's graduating class of 1994 and with friends and family proudly looking on, Calvin received an honourary doctorate of law.

"I was walking with him because I had nominated him," explains Joan, "and he was from our school and I was carrying this small little binder and I thought it had his speech in it. Just before he was going to give his remarks, I leaned over to him and said, 'Calvin, I have this.' He had asked me to carry it. He said, 'Oh no, I don't need that.' So I put it under my chair again and gave it to him at the end of the ceremony. But as far as I can see he never referenced anything."

As Doug explains, the binder was more of a "security blanket" and there was probably no speech inside. "We've always had this thing if you're going to a meeting, if you're going somewhere, you always have some paper or something with you. Just in case. Just in case a meeting breaks out," Doug laughs as he thinks about the possibility of having to take notes while receiving an honourary degree. "Dad never believed he would be anywhere unprepared. So even when you're giving him an honourary degree and you're giving a convocation address, you had something with paper, just in case he had to make notes. If I'm going somewhere, I always have my briefcase with me. It's just a natural thing and I got that from my father."

As Calvin approached the podium to address the audience, he did something that Joan says was a first for any convocation ceremony she's ever attended. While Calvin was being honoured he wanted to take a moment to honour his friends and family, so he named each family member one by one, and one by one, whether they wanted to or not, they stood up upon Calvin's instruction.

"Most people don't do this," admits Joan. "Most people when they get an honourary degree, they're up and they're starting to give their remarks. And Calvin before he started to give his remarks he introduced Joyce and Doug and Martin and I think there were friends. But it was lovely. Everything was warmed up by Calvin. I had never seen it before and I went to many, many convocations and saw people get honourary degrees. But that was Calvin. He really warmed the whole ceremony up."

When Calvin did begin to speak, one of the youngest members of the Ruck family remembers taking notice and realizing that this man who drove her to school every day while her father was ill really was special. Jacqueline was ten years old at the time.

"I remember that was the first speech he gave that I started to tear up because I realized this man has had so many struggles and been confronted with so much racism, but yet the person he presented to me was always with a smile on his face, so I wouldn't have known those things from just him driving me to school because he was always happy. That's when I realized this man was something special and was doing something special."

8: Triumph And Tragedy

Robert Maxwell, who had seen the tremendous progress and strides Calvin had made since their initial meeting at CFB Shearwater, put Calvin's name forward to receive Canada's highest civilian honour – the Order of Canada. "I thought he was truly deserving. What he accomplished benefitted his community, province, and country." The Order of Canada "recognizes a lifetime of outstanding achievement, dedication to the community and service to the nation," and the motto inscribed on the medal of honour states: *Desiderantes Meliorem Patriam* (They desire a better country) – a fitting definition of Calvin.

"I saw just what a tremendous time of change the '60s, '70s and '80s were," recalls Bridglal Pachai. "Those were the decades of principal change in Nova Scotia, and he was a very strong leader articulating a vision for the future from the '60s onwards. He never removed himself from that philosophy that we are making improvements."

In 1994, it was announced Calvin would receive the Order of Canada, and he attended the investiture ceremony in Ottawa in May 1995. The ceremony permits the recipient to bring only one guest. Naturally, Joyce was by Calvin's side.

While the dress code has since changed, the formal affair required Calvin purchase his first tuxedo, a look he pulled off effortlessly. Joyce, who also stole the show in a long blue evening gown, recalls her shopping experience at Mills Brothers in Halifax. Terri Gray and best friend Phyllis

Lucas accompanied Joyce to find the perfect outfit. "They said I was very fussy," says Joyce with a smile. "I was a hard person to please and I didn't like everything I tried on."

A car picked Calvin and Joyce up at the Fairmont Château Laurier, located in downtown Ottawa, and brought them to Rideau Hall. "We all went into this big room with chandeliers hanging down," recalls Joyce. "They put Calvin in the front because his eyesight wasn't very good and they called each person's name out."

Calvin shook hands with Governor General Roméo LeBlanc, signed his name and posed for photos. Following the ceremony, he and Joyce attended a dinner and reception. While Calvin remained humble no matter what happened in his life, his family could not have been prouder and it once again reminded them that Calvin started with very little and through determination and integrity, he accomplished so much.

"I think we have a lot to be proud of," Darren Ruck says of his uncle, "when you consider the fact that he never finished high school. Considering the time and the racism that existed and the barriers that would have been against him, to accomplish what he did would have been no easy feat. What do we have to complain about when you consider what was against him? I'm pretty proud of the family. There's a sense of obligation to do the best you can because you're a part of this family. Treat it as an asset but don't take it for granted."

Word of Calvin's national recognition was celebrated by family and friends around the world – including their daughter Rochelle (Shelley), who was living in Australia. Rochelle communicated with her parents through phone calls and letters. Like her father, Rochelle had great energy and vision, although her gifts were of a different kind. She would update them on her most recent fashion and acting opportunities and send photos and newspaper clippings of things happening in her neighbourhood. Joyce would do the same, filling her in on Calvin's current projects and honours received and also sharing photos of the pair at ceremonies and events. In several letters, Rochelle mentioned receiving these photos and letters from her parents were the favourite part of her day. From drawing and painting to clothing design, Rochelle was an artist and saw beauty in the rarest of places.

"She was so very artistic," says Doug, "and she had to express it. One of her biggest passions as a child was drawing. She started drawing clothing when she was very young. She was very talented. We would both draw constantly." The three Ruck children shared a bedroom in the basement and Doug says he and his sister would spend hours in their room drawing. "Dad would bring paper and stuff home from Shearwater when he was working there. Sometimes it was just scrap paper but it was like a luxury for us. I'm drawing these creatures and stick figures and Shelley's doing these amazing drawings. She could see them in her mind and draw them."

Valerie was friends with Rochelle before she met Doug. "She was unique. She had a whole different mindset. She liked to create things. She didn't dress like anybody because she only wore clothes that she had made."

As the only Black children in the neigbourhood, Doug describes Rochelle as his best friend, and the two spent a lot of time together when there was no one else who they could associate with. "She knew how to say things just to irritate me. She would tease me terribly just to get on my nerves. But growing up as children we were each other's best friends. Because we were the only Black kids in the neighbourhood, I was very protective of her. There was a very real sensitivity there."

Craving independence, Rochelle left Walker Street at a young age and started her own path and her own life in Vancouver, later moving to Toronto. The Ruck family didn't get to see her as much as they would have liked, which made her visits that much more special. "When she visited or when we visited Toronto I wanted to be by her side every second," says Rochelle's niece Jacqueline. "I did not want to leave her side. I thought she was gorgeous. She was talented. She would make me clothes. She would make me scarves. I just loved her. I think had she lived in Halifax, I would have been much closer to her because I just loved any time I got to spend with her."

While living in Toronto in 1976, Rochelle wrote a letter to Joyce and Calvin, informing them she had been diagnosed with sarcoidosis, a disease that leads to inflammation in the body's organs. She was in her twenties at the time. "When she lived in Toronto, after the diagnosis, she couldn't be overly strenuous," recalls Doug. "If she was walking she would have to stop to take her breath." While the onset was gradual, Rochelle's symptoms began to worsen.

In July 1992, Rochelle and her long-time partner, Michael Wearne, decided to move to Australia to be closer to Michael's family. While the couple looked forward to their new life, Joyce was not comfortable with her daughter going so far away. Upon word of Rochelle's illness, Joyce already felt helpless not having her daughter nearby, so Rochelle's moving halfway across the world filled Joyce with worry and concern as she could not say when she would see her daughter again.

Rochelle's life in Australia was filled with creativity and love. She was still designing beautiful works of art and had been adopted, so to speak, by Michael's family. "Michael's family thought the world of her," says Doug. "It was a large family. She would design clothing for the younger kids. She had a certain freedom in Australia to explore her artistic side. When I would talk to her, she would talk about enjoying it. She would talk about going to the beach for a barbecue on Christmas Day."

Not having a furnace combined with damp air worsened Rochelle's symptoms and she was eventually placed on permanent breathing tubes. One evening after being out with friends, Joyce's mother's intuition became overwhelming and she knew she had to call her daughter. After receiving no answer at home and calling around, Joyce found out that her daughter had been taken to the hospital. She was eventually put through to Rochelle. "She was out of breath but she tried to act like everything was fine," recalls Joyce.

Rochelle's survival was dependant on a double lung and heart transplant. Her family was hopeful. "I expected that she would get it," admits Doug. "I had no doubt that she would get it. So when the news came, it came as a shock." On February 6, 1996, at forty-three years of age, Rochelle passed away with her Australian friends and family by her side. A beautiful life was taken too soon.

"When Aunt Shelley passed away my initial response was anger," acknowledges Jacqueline. "I was very, very mad. Because it seemed and still seems very unfair that a life be taken that young. It was my first time being confronted with death, so I was confused and I was angry."

Rochelle Ruck.

Jacqueline also saw a side of her father she had not seen before. "I remember seeing him more vulnerable than I've ever seen him and it was strange for me. I guess part of growing up is realizing that your parents are human and it's not really a lesson I've enjoyed learning because if they're feeling weak, how am I supposed to feel? That made me angrier that this was happening because you don't want to see someone you love hurt and upset."

The pain of losing a loved one is heartbreaking enough, but Joyce and Calvin also had to deal with the fact that just months before, they had talked about visiting Rochelle in Australia. The couple shared their travel plans over the phone with their daughter. In a letter, Rochelle expressed her excitement at the news, calling it the "best day of my life."

Calvin and Joyce had lost their only daughter, and although Jacqueline saw that raw emotion of sadness and despair in her father, she never saw it in her grandfather. The only person who did witness Calvin's pain was Joyce, who encouraged her husband to release the emotion he was harbouring inside, and she was there to comfort him when he finally took her advice. "I didn't see Granddad cry and Nanny told me that she spoke to him and said that she knows that he doesn't want to cry right now, but it's important to just let it out because you need to release that pain."

Calvin, Joyce, Doug, and Martin flew to Australia, on a thirty-three-hour flight, to say their final goodbyes to their daughter and sister. "I can still see him sitting on the plane with his Lions cap on," says Doug when thinking of Calvin. "He had me call the Sydney Lions Club and spoke to the president about the Nova Scotia Lions Club. He was very proud of the Lions."

To add to the stress and emotion of that trip, Calvin had recently been declared legally blind and he was slowly losing his complete independence. "It was a difficult time for Dad," says Doug. "He was just adjusting to not being able to see. His emotion was that his daughter had died which was very, very difficult. At the same time, she died in a foreign country away from him. Dad wasn't one who showed a huge outpouring of emotion, but I know it was tough."

This was the first time the Rucks had been to Australia and the first time they would meet the people who got to see Rochelle every day and saw her as one of their own. "It took a lot out of me," says Joyce. "When I got to Australia, I had to comfort them. Everybody was crying and then I came home and I broke down and I cried for days and Calvin would come downstairs and try to calm me down."

At the funeral, Doug shared his emotions about coming to Australia to, in a sense, bring his sister back. "Going there, I really had no idea what things were really like for Shelley until I started talking to people and I saw all the love. I went there to in some way bring my sister's spirit home with us, but after being there and talking to people, I realized this was where she belonged. The sadness I had felt not being with her when she died was still there, but not in the same way that she was alone because it was far from that. The same way that people talk about how Dad has had an impact on their lives was the same way they talked about her. The joy she brought into it; the kindness she brought into it."

While Doug found closure in Australia, he says there will always be a part of his sister with him. "After going to Australia, there's a part of her that's not gone. She's still there with me. I know she's not there in a physical sense, but her impact is always there. Being around her taught me about colours and how things blended. Shelley didn't believe in staying in the lines. To me, blue jeans were blue. Shoes were brown or black. My picture would be perfect to me because I would stay inside the lines, but it wasn't artistic the way Shelley's was. Hers had a feeling to it. Shelley had the person wearing orange shoes and purple pants. She taught me to go outside the lines."

Joyce says the pain of losing a child was overwhelming to say the least and it took a great amount of time before life went back to something approaching normal. "On Mother's Day she always sent me a card. I didn't really like Mother's Day to come anymore. My best friend Phyllis said, 'You must remember that you have other children.' I wasn't going to have Christmas; I didn't want to celebrate anything. It was a long while, but all of a sudden things seemed to fall back in place. That was the hardest time in my life."

9: Senator Ruck

With reduced vision, Calvin was beginning to do more things around the house, such as gardening. He was constantly planting and grooming, to bring new life to his backyard. He loved the beauty of flowers and the satisfaction of seeing his hard work bloom and flourish. He built his own flower boxes, dug gardening plots around his yard and shared his work with whoever came for a visit. "He took a lot of pride in the presentation of his lawn," recalls Jacqueline. "That was the only thing I can think of that he did for him. That was his hobby, what he enjoyed doing."

Besides gardening, he also had more time to begin work on his second book, which focused on the Second World War. His research skills were put back into motion, as he collected document upon document concerning Black soldiers during World War II. He also began to contact family members of the veterans and receive pictures of the soldiers who would bring his book to life. His home had also become his office.

In a drafted introduction to the book, with a working title of "Blacks in World War Two: They Also Served King and Country," Calvin wrote:

> *History is defined in numerous ways. The Oxford Advanced Learners Dictionary defines history as a study of past events, especially the political, social and economic development of a country, a continent or the world. For the*

purposes of this paper, we will examine the Black experience in WWII from a number of perspectives.

In terms of military conflict on a worldwide basis, history tells us that the First World War ended on November 11, 1918 at the eleventh hour on the eleventh day of the eleventh month. The guns ceased firing. The Great War was over. It had been described as the war to end all wars. However that exaggerated hope was only rhetoric.

Twenty-one years later on September 1, 1939, the world was again at war. Canada officially became a participant in WWII on September 10, 1939.

Historical records indicate that Black Canadians have played a role in every major military engagement during the past 200 years that Canada, as a British colony and as a sovereign nation, has participated in. Black Canadians have patriotically participated in all of these wars and conflicts. However, military historians and writers in general have consistently ignored the roles played.

… we will examine the Black experience from several perspectives, including the historical context, the social implications, the attitudes prevailing the military service aspect in terms of the roles performed and the post war years. We will also examine the recruiting policies of the navy and air force.

From the outset, permit me to quote from a book by Leo W. Bertley – Canada and its People of African Descent, concerning World War One and World War Two. He wrote: Not much had changed between the great wars, racism was in business in 1940 as in 1914.

As he delved further into his research, it seemed that Bertley's words had been correct. Calvin began uncovering forgotten anecdotes of those Black men who served their country but went unnoticed in history books.

On pieces of scrap paper in capital letters (due to his failing sight), Calvin wrote of William Hall, who went above and beyond the call of duty and yet was considered a nobody because of the colour of his skin. Hall (1827-1904) was awarded the Victoria Cross in 1859, following his heroic actions in the Sepoy Rebellion in India in 1857. Even upon death, Hall's heroics were belittled and unappreciated.

> *William Hall was the first Black man, the first Nova Scotian and the first Canadian sailor to win the British Empire's highest award for bravery – the Victoria Cross. The fact that William Hall was a Black man appears to have been a source of embarrassment for civilian and military officials. There is no evidence that he received any Canadian recognition for his tremendous service to King and country. To some degree, he can still be classified as the unknown hero. As a matter of fact, the clergyman conducting Hall's funeral service referred to him as a brave man, who as a child was a pickaninny not unlike other pickaninnies.*

Another man who Calvin kept extensive documents on was Piercy Haynes. Following his report on Hall, Calvin began to tell Haynes' story:

> *In June 1942, the blatant racist policy of excluding Blacks from the Navy was challenged by a Black man, Piercy Haynes, from Winnipeg, Man. An interesting exchange of letters ensued between Mr. Haynes and the minister of National Defence, the Honourable Angus L. Macdonald [a former premier of Nova Scotia]. On June 13, Haynes, after being refused because of his race wrote to Mr. Macdonald, and in no uncertain terms, made it very clear that Canada was not living up to its professed democratic ideals. In the opening paragraph he wrote: It is with sincere regret that I am forced to write this letter. I find that the teachings of the democratic world, the democracy for which we are fighting are mere words and a menace to ourselves when they cannot be practised by our own military forces.*

With a photocopy of it in hand, Calvin recorded Macdonald's response, written by his private secretary, to Haynes:

> Mr. Macdonald has asked me to acknowledge your letter of the 13th of June, with regard to the entry of coloured personnel in the Royal Canadian Navy. I may say that so far as service in the RCN is concerned, one of the conditions of entry is that candidates must be of the white race. You will understand that this provision is made in the interests of those not of the white race.
>
> Long experience has shown that where a large percentage of any body of men is of one race, it is not advisable to require those of another race to serve with them. This provision is made wholly for the well-being of the minority and is based on known conditions of well-being only.

It is no surprise that Haynes did not see the validity in this argument and was not ready to accept the explanation. Upon further communication and a review of the Naval Order concerning "coloured personnel," Haynes finally received a letter of response on March 26, 1943, from that same secretary, on behalf of Mr. Macdonald:

> Mr. Macdonald has asked me to acknowledge your telegram of the 26th of March, and to say that he is very pleased that your application for entry into the Service has been accepted.

On a Post-it note stuck to a piece of scrap paper, Calvin wrote, "Petty Officer Piercey [sic] A. Haynes the first black to be accepted into the R.C.N."

Calvin began compiling these stories, marking important dates and making lists of possible contacts and veteran family members who may be able to help piece the story together of Black soldiers in World War Two. While Calvin's second book was slowly coming together, his eyesight was failing and his ability to research and go through numerous documents became difficult. He no longer had the luxury of just getting into the car and driving to a meeting or spending hours at the library.

With Calvin spending more time at home, people were constantly calling the Ruck household to speak to him. Whether it was for an interview for a local media network, for aid involving a social issue, or to speak to Calvin concerning a committee he was associated with, he was always ready to deal with whatever the telephone ring might bring. In 1998, however, Calvin got a phone call he was not ready for.

A staff member in Prime Minister Jean Chrétien's office in Ottawa was calling to see if Calvin Ruck's name could go on a short list of potential candidates from Nova Scotia to be appointed to the Senate.

"I had no idea at all what the short list was. It [politics] was all brand new to me. As my wife often says, I am not a political person." Unsure of how to respond, Calvin told the man he had to think about it and discuss it further with his wife. The discussion didn't last long, though, as Joyce recalls not taking the offer very seriously when he first approached her about the idea of becoming a senator. "I was sleeping at the time when that first phone call came. He came into the room and told me about the offer. Right away I just told him not to be so ridiculous and that he was not political." With that being said, Calvin and Joyce didn't think much more about it as they had become quite content with their lives.

They had been living at the same address for more than thirty years. Nova Scotia was their home, and despite the honour, they were unsure if they wanted to make the change. "It is not an easy matter to just close your house, put a lock on the door and go off," Calvin told his fellow senators when discussing his appointment. This was apparent when a second phone call came from the Prime Minister's Office to see if they had come to any conclusions. Once again, Calvin wasn't ready to accept just yet, and neither was Joyce. "I had no desire to go to Ottawa," says Joyce. "I didn't know anyone up there and Calvin had never been involved with politics before."

Although Calvin did not view himself as a political man, this was not the first time others had. He was once approached to run as a member of the New Democratic Party (NDP). He politely turned it down, saying his reasoning was that he "didn't like to lose." He also stated that he was too busy doing work in the community to devote his time to a political party. Both responses in this case, however, were not valid, as he was being appointed to the Senate, not elected, and he was not as consistently active as he used to be.

Calvin's biggest concern or reason for hesitation was his eyesight. He was unsure if he would be able to perform daily tasks with his vision continuing to decrease. It was not until a third phone call to the Ruck residence that Calvin decided he and his wife would make the move to the nation's capital. "A telephone call came from the Prime Minister himself," Calvin wrote in an address to the Senate. "It is quite an honour to have the Prime Minister call. I put him on hold for a brief period while I was still thinking about it."

This decision came to be after a small but confident push from their son, Doug, who also lived in Dartmouth with his wife and two children. When Joyce told her son of the offer, Doug was confused as to why his parents were taking so long to decide. "I didn't understand why there was any hesitation to accept the position at all. It was an amazing opportunity. It was something that he should do, not only because it was important to be done, but also because it was something he deserved. My parents made a lot of sacrifices for us [children]. They worked hard to ensure we were fed and clothed. They both deserved this." He assured his parents he would look after the house, as they would be travelling back and forth. He also assured them the Senate would make sure to accommodate Calvin, so his eyesight would not be a worry or affect his work.

News travelled quickly of the third Black person (after Anne Clare Cools in 1984 and Donald Oliver in 1990) appointed to the Senate of Canada. Headlines read, "N.S. Black activist appointed to Senate" and "New Senator beat the odds." Newspapers across the country began reporting his early struggle to find housing for his family and highlighting his accomplishments as an activist and a social worker.

When *The Chronicle Herald* asked her about Calvin's appointment, former NDP leader Alexa McDonough stated, "If the Senate was filled with Calvin Rucks, it would be worthy of a great deal of respect from Canadians." Calvin's Nova Scotian community was now waiting to see what he would do and Calvin was determined, as always, to once again blow the winds of change. So in the summer of 1998, seventy-three-year-old Calvin, with Joyce by his side, flew to Ottawa. "I wasn't nervous going to Ottawa because I was with him," says Joyce. "He was a man that made you feel at ease."

"I never called him Calvin after that or Mr. Ruck," says Henry Bishop, who always refers to Calvin as Senator or Dr. Ruck, and who coined the phrase 'From janitor to senator.' "I knew he had earned it."

On a hot summer day, Calvin was sworn in to the Senate of Canada. The day was filled with excitement and support from his immediate family and friends. Doug and his family travelled from Dartmouth to Ottawa, and Calvin's youngest son, Martin, flew in from Toronto. Fourteen at the time, Jacqueline remembers the day proudly.

"It was a whirlwind. I got into Ottawa the morning that he was sworn in. We took a tour of the Parliament Buildings and actually saw Jean Chrétien, who just happened to be walking by. Next thing I know, that night I was watching Granddad walk into the Senate chamber and then be sworn in. It was a lot to take in, especially for someone so young. But it was exciting, it was happy and it was a proud day."

As the family watched Calvin walk down the long Chamber Hall, Doug couldn't help but think that not that long ago, the only way his father would be walking down that hall was if he was cleaning after hours. Calvin was actively living out what he had fought so long for. It was a proud moment for the Ruck family as they sat in the gallery above and watched their loved one being sworn in.

That same summer, Calvin and Joyce had something else to celebrate – their fiftieth wedding anniversary. The family would mark the occasion together at a much-anticipated Ruck reunion, taking place in Calvin's hometown of Sydney. Over forty friends and family members gathered, some meeting for the very first time. In a special presentation to the couple, Joyce and Calvin were presented with letters of congratulations from the Prime Minister and the Governor General.

"You could tell that Joyce respected him," says Terri Gray. "However, she didn't let him get away with too much. Like if he said something, her comment would be 'Oh Calvin, be quiet, Calvin.' But you could tell that they had a love for each other that was just understood."

After taking in a well-deserved dose of home, Calvin and Joyce returned to Ottawa to prepare for Calvin's first session in the Senate. In an interview with the *Ottawa Citizen*, Calvin told the reporter about the inspiration Dr. Martin Luther King, Jr. had on his life and how he had been "greatly affected" by the Civil Rights Movement in the United States. "I thought we should take a cue from the people in the States and stand up for our rights. Feelings of inferiority lead to fear. If you don't have fear, then you make your voice heard." Another hero of Calvin's knew too well the effects of making his voice heard, and on Thursday, September 24, 1998, these two men were going to meet for the first time.

Calvin was constantly researching and filing information on historical events or important players in the human rights movement. One of these folders was specifically designated for the former president of South Africa, Nelson Mandela. Calvin looked to Mandela's published words for inspiration and motivation, stating his favourite book to be *The Long Walk to Freedom*, Mandela's autobiography. "This book is on the top of my list. Mandela strove hard for the human rights of Blacks in South Africa. Despite his incarceration for so many years, he still seemed to speak out from his cell. When he was finally released, he held no hatred for his captors … and went on to lead his country. Nelson Mandela is truly a remarkable man."

Calvin's assistant, Cheryl Hannaford, informed him that Mandela would be coming to Ottawa for a visit. Although she had not known her new boss for very long, she knew that if anyone should meet Nelson Mandela, it should be the man who knew more about human rights issues than anyone else she had ever met. The Prime Minster felt the same way and invited Calvin to the House when Mandela gave his address to Canada. Joyce sat in the gallery and listened as Prime Minister Jean Chrétien introduced a man Calvin had looked to for motivation: "Your struggle was an inspiration to freedom-loving men and women everywhere. But, in a sense, the courage, optimism and generosity of spirit you have shown after your struggle have been even more of an inspiration. That suffering does not only lead to bitterness and disillusion; it can lead to wisdom and compassion. And to a better world. Ladies and gentlemen, I am honoured to present to you the leader of his nation, the statesman of his continent, and a hero for the world. President Nelson Mandela."

Mandela's first address to the Parliament of Canada came eight years before as a freedom fighter who was denied citizenship in his own country. This time, he was standing before them as an elected representative of the South African people. He spoke of the changes he has seen in his country and also admitted that equality does not yet reign supreme.

> We have therefore been able to make a good start in bringing basic amenities to millions of people for the first time in their lives: electricity, clean water, health care facilities, housing and schooling.
> We do face major challenges and problems. What is important is that we are confronting them and we are confident that we will overcome them.

Following Mandela's address, Joyce and Calvin were escorted into the hall, where photographers and journalists flooded the area. "There were so many people," Joyce recalls. "I didn't know which way to look." It wasn't long before Chrétien and Mandela were approaching the Rucks in that crowded hallway. Chrétien had said that he wanted the African president to meet Senator Ruck. The two shook hands and exchanged polite chatter.

That same evening, Calvin and Joyce attended a banquet of one hundred guests at Rideau Hall, held in honour of Canada's African visitor and his wife. Once again, Calvin and Mandela were shaking hands. This time, Joyce was able to meet his wife, Graça Machel. Unbeknownst to Joyce, Graça Machel had already seen her earlier that day. "She shook my hand and said that she had already noticed me when I was sitting up in the gallery, because I was the only Black person up there." The Rucks were once again being singled out for being different, but this time, it was in their favour.

Reflecting on the meeting, Calvin described it as "a moment I will never forget." He would later mention Mandela, his inspiration, in an address to the Senate:

> I like the phrase the winds of change, which people use when speaking about human rights. The remark was coined by the late Sir Harold MacMillan when he was prime

minister of Great Britain. He pleaded with the people of South Africa to recognize the winds of change. His words fell on deaf ears. However, Nelson Mandela then came onto the stage and they literally wiped out those people who did not see them as equal persons.

What better way of welcoming a man into the Senate than by having him meet one of his heroes. Calvin was now certain he had made the right decision to come to Ottawa, and he was ready and inspired to roll up his sleeves and get to work.

Calvin had the encouragement of a community behind him and he was reminded of that support daily, as notes of congratulations poured in for the newly appointed senator. "It is long overdue that you be given this status and without a doubt I can't think of anyone else that deserves it more," wrote Henry Bishop. "It is a proud day for you and the Black community also to have you receive this prestigious post. It shows that good things happen to those that wait and your continuous hard work has finally paid off."

In a reply of thanks, Calvin confirmed that he would be representing his beloved province and taking advantage of this larger platform: "While my time in Ottawa will be short [because of the Senate's mandatory retirement age of seventy-five], I am looking forward to this new experience, and will take full advantage of this national forum to work on behalf of my community and all the people of Nova Scotia."

When first arriving in the nation's capital, Senator Ruck was on Parliament Hill every day, and it didn't take long for him to find his footing in Ottawa. He fit in quite well with his peers and had made a name for himself in the Senate. Whenever given the chance to speak, Calvin used the opportunity to talk about the struggles and injustices that had and still faced Black Canadians. He didn't waste any time addressing one particular issue – the case of the fallen Black veterans' unmarked burial sites.

"Some years ago, my wife and I buried my brother-in-law. When we went to the undertaker's parlour, he called Camp Hill Cemetery and said – and I will never forget his words – 'Open a grave in the Black section' or 'the coloured section.' I am not sure what term they were using in those days. We were known as coloured and now we hear the word Black used most of the time. Anyway, we did not offer any objection. We wanted to bury our brother-in-law in a grave and we did not have a lot of money. He had been unemployed for a number of years and had no insurance, so we had to come to some agreement. Therefore, I did not make an issue over the term coloured or Black. It was the first we knew that there was such a thing as a Black or coloured section in Camp Hill Cemetery, one of the main cemeteries in the City of Halifax. He was buried there.

"Subsequently, I became involved with the history of the Black Battalion and I read that some Black veterans of that battalion were buried in unmarked graves. I went to the cemetery myself and I saw the graves there. I did not pursue the matter at that time, but we are now living in an age where people are people, to be judged by their nature, not by the colour of their skin."

While Calvin's book, *The Black Battalion 1916-1920: Canada's Best Kept Military Secret*, gave soldiers the initial recognition they deserved, the men were still not recognized properly on tombstones. They were buried in Camp Hill Cemetery and marked by flat, white stones, making it impossible for anyone to know that any bodies were even in the area. Such recognition was not given as no one at the time had the money or desire to give these men proper plots. Calvin decided that his seat in the Senate was now the perfect podium for his cause. He began by sitting on the sub-committee for Veterans Affairs. His first year in the Senate, Calvin gave a speech informing his colleagues of the matter and what he was doing to try to ensure these gentlemen received proper gravestones. Like all of the other issues Calvin had dealt with before, he had faith that this too would change. "One hopes that this matter will be rectified and those veterans of World War I who served and fought so that we may survive as a country will get the honour they deserve, a marker that can be seen without groping the grass."

That same year, Calvin received word from the Department of Veterans Affairs office in Halifax that the approval had been given for the placement of proper headstones at the burial site of Black veterans at the Halifax cemetery. Over the Christmas recess, Calvin, with the aid of others involved in Veterans Affairs, worked hard to contact the families of the deceased veterans to let them know what was happening and to inquire as to what their wishes were for the new headstones. On December 9, 1998, in a letter, Calvin thanked the then minister of Veterans Affairs, Fred Mifflin, for his support throughout the process: "Mr. Minister, please accept my heartfelt thanks for the quick and positive action you have taken with regard to this matter, and for the respect which you have shown towards these men, who, too often, have been forgotten."

Not a year after arriving in the Senate, Calvin had already accomplished one of his main goals. His continuous effort, however, to educate as well as motivate never stopped.

Newly appointed senators in 1998: left to right are Marian L. Maloney, Frank Mahovlich, Rev. Lois Wilson, Richard Croft, and Calvin.

10: No Place Like Home

While Calvin was working on Parliament Hill, Joyce kept herself busy, adjusting quickly to her new life in Ottawa. "I would be busy, cooking his meals, getting his clothes ready for the next day and we would go grocery shopping together. There was always something to do." Joyce also attended meetings for the spouses' association, a monthly get-together at the Speaker's house.

While Calvin was making strides in Ottawa, his son Doug was also making waves back home, carrying out his duties as the first Black ombudsman for Nova Scotia. In an address to the chamber, Calvin used his son's breakthrough to once again speak to the value of education, not to mention how proud he was as a father.

"The provincial ombudsman in Nova Scotia is a young Black man who happens to be my son, Douglas Ruck. He was the first Black person in Nova Scotia, to the best of my knowledge, to receive such an honour. He spent some time speaking to people here in Ottawa about setting up a national organization of that type. He has travelled around quite a bit.

"The winds of change are blowing throughout Nova Scotia in respect of both eligibility and consideration of people. We can do the job provided that we are given the opportunity and provided that we are treated as equals. That is happening. There have been major improvements. Many of our young people, male and female, are going on to university and ending up with good jobs. That is basically where we are. We keep telling our young people to stay in school, to get an education and to make a contribution to the development of our province and our country."

Calvin knew he was blessed to now be in the position he was in and he also knew that many Black men will never have the same opportunities. Many Black men will never set foot in the halls of the Parliament Buildings and will never feel as important or deserving as perhaps they should. For at least one night, Calvin wanted to change that. He began to plan an evening for twelve Black Canadians. The idea for such an occasion stemmed from an organization formed by Robert Maxwell – the Black Military Personnel Organization. "I had been invited to Washington on one occasion and attended a meeting of U.S. Black military officers. I felt the same should take place in Canada." In 1998, the lieutenant-colonel called together Black military personnel to a meeting in Ottawa to discuss common goals and objectives. He also invited Calvin to attend the inaugural meeting. "It was his presence that made the meetings a success and kept peoples' interest," he says. After attending later meetings, Calvin welcomed the organization to Parliament Hill.

Joyce had invited friends from Dartmouth to join her for dinner that evening and as she sat on the sixth floor, she remembers looking down and seeing Calvin. "While I was up there, there was Calvin with his white cane and all of these Black men behind him." The men enjoyed a catered meal in the Parliamentary Restaurant and just enjoyed being in each other's company.

While Calvin set out to honour others, Henry Bishop organized an evening to honour Calvin – calling it Night of the Senator. On the night of October 17, 1998, which also marked the fifteenth anniversary of the Black Cultural Centre, more than 250 people of all creeds and colours filled the Centre to celebrate this man of integrity. Everything Calvin did in Ottawa was relayed back to his many friends and family in Nova Scotia and this was their way of celebrating with him.

Once everyone had taken their seats, the evening began with a procession of dignitaries led by a pipe-and-drum band. Calvin donned a black tuxedo, and with Joyce proudly by his side, the couple was welcomed home with an entrance fit for a king. Many stepped up to the podium to express their admiration for Calvin's life work. Among them were former lieutenant-governor J. James Kinley and former premier of Nova Scotia Russell MacLellan, who called Calvin one of the icons of Nova Scotia.

As a nod to Calvin's love of music, Bucky Adams, known as the Black Prince of Jazz, along with other musical guests, entertained the crowd. Also honouring her grandfather through song, Jacqueline sang "His Strength is Perfect," a fitting choice as Calvin, no matter what he did, always gave all glory to God.

Standing just a few feet away from the Centre's exhibit on the No. 2 Construction Battalion, actor and close family friend Anthony Sherwood, creator of *Honour Before Glory*, the docudrama on the No. 2, spoke of Calvin's character in the keynote address. "I think his humility and his generosity are two of his strongest characteristics. He gives to the community pride – he's given so much of his heart and soul to the community."

Calvin's humility was apparent as he spoke to the many family, friends and colleagues who had gathered. "You don't foresee these things happening, but when they happen, it creates a few butterflies seeing all the folks here."

Doug also spoke of how proud he was of his father and shared his thoughts on seeing Calvin as he walked down the halls of Parliament. "I guess that in some ways at that age I was looking to Dad to know what was important and know what to take note of," says Jacqueline when reflecting on her father's words. "To know what I was supposed to pause and let sink in. And when Dad gave that perfectly worded speech, it did sink in just how remarkable it is that a Black man has been appointed to the Senate."

It is clear that Doug's gift of oration stems directly from his father. Even before his Senate appointment, Calvin was constantly called upon to speak to groups, big and small, in various communities. In November of 1998, Calvin received a request to speak at a Remembrance Day ceremony in Sydney. Although also invited to attend the ceremony in Ottawa, Calvin told the people of Sydney his decision to pay his respects in Nova Scotia was an easy one, stating, "It's always good to return home."

Calvin shared the story of those Black men who were denied the right to fight alongside white soldiers during the war, describing their service in the No. 2 Construction Battalion as "valiant." Calvin then invited Doug to call out the names of those fallen Black soldiers who had died overseas. *The Cape Breton Post* reports that Calvin's words were received with a standing ovation.

In December 1998, the Senate recognized the fiftieth anniversary of the signing of the Universal Declaration of Human Rights. Spending decades fighting for minority rights, Calvin knew he wanted to publicly speak about this half-century milestone. It was also a chance for the newly appointed senator to share with his peers, some who still probably knew little of his background, his very personal battle with the concept of equality and human rights.

"That declaration has had a personal effect on my life as a member of a minority group. The opening chapter states that all men are created equal, and they are endowed by their Creator with certain inalienable rights, and among these are life, liberty, and the pursuit of happiness. Those words do not always apply to minority persons, as many of you are aware.

"We have seen many changes come about since the declaration. We have seen the Government of Canada set up a Human Rights Commission. We have seen the various provinces set up human rights commissions. This has opened many doors to visible minorities. There were times previous to that when we as visible minorities could not go into barbershops in the city of Dartmouth, and many other cities in Nova Scotia. I cannot speak for other parts of Canada, but I know we in Nova Scotia have benefitted immensely from that declaration.

"I was able to purchase land that previously had been declared out of bounds to members of the Black community. I was able to raise a family there and see that they were properly educated. My oldest son went on to become a lawyer, and he is now the provincial ombudsman for the Province of Nova Scotia, so you can see how that declaration has impacted on the rights, privileges, and opportunities of minority persons.

"The winds of change are blowing throughout this country, and the declaration has had a major impact with respect to those winds. We have come a long ways. We can now go into barbershops in the city of

Dartmouth. It took a number of years before I was admitted, but human rights law brought that into being. In theatres in some parts of Nova Scotia, we could only sit in the balcony. They had a phrase for that, but I will not use that phrase right now. Doors have opened. Things have improved. We now have many members of our community working in department stores and in banks as bank clerks. There was a time when we could not borrow money from banks, much less work in a bank.

"Things have changed. I thank God. I am proud to be a Canadian. Our country has come a long ways, but there is still some ways to go. My presence here indicates some of the changes that have taken place. Minority people have become members of parliament. Not too many years ago that was unheard of, so progress has been made, and I am very proud to stand here this afternoon."

Staying in tune with his human rights background, Calvin joined the Senate Human Rights Committee in his second year in Ottawa.

Not yet taking the opportunity to elaborate on his research regarding the Black Battalion, Calvin decided to share with his peers the story he had been telling for so many years. He wanted them to understand why he fought so hard for these Black veterans and he saw it fit to educate and remind his fellow senators of the fight and struggle of Black men trying to enlist to serve their country. Calvin was a historian and a storyteller, so on Wednesday, March 10, 1999, Calvin stood up, white cane in hand, and told a story.

"Honourable senators, please bear with me. As the white cane indicates, I am a legally blind person. Also, on occasion, I suffer from memory loss. I thank you for staying around for my speech. It has been a long session and I will try to be as brief as possible.

"Let us go back in time a bit. The era I am talking about is a bit prior to World War I. The year is 1910. The government of Sir Wilfrid Laurier, in common with people throughout the world, is preparing for World War I. One of the first steps, according to what I have read in history, is with respect to the naval service. It appeared at that point in time that Canada did not possess a navy, so the government of Sir Wilfrid Laurier passed an act creating, at least on paper, a branch of the service we once proudly referred to as the Royal Canadian Navy.

"Let us go a little further along the agenda, with respect to the rules and regulations which were brought in not too long after the act was passed. The first clause of the rules and regulations states explicitly that all recruits must be members of the white race.

"Human rights have done a lot to change that kind of attitude. Now Blacks, native persons, Indians, Chinese, Japanese, whatever, are in the Armed Forces regardless of their race. We have come a long way. I have no animosity. I am not here today to embarrass anyone over what happened in 1910. With the human rights legislation we have in place, that sort of thing could not happen again. Black people and other minority groups are proud to serve their country. They demonstrated that in World War II, despite the roadblocks."

Calvin also shared a story of Nova Scotian Allan Bundy. His application was turned down for enrollment into the air force during World War II. Bundy did not dispute the matter and went home, planning on putting the incident behind him. Not long after, an RCMP officer knocked on his door because he had not responded to a request to enlist in the army. Bundy had no plans to enlist in the army after being rejected by the air force, so he told the officer to arrest him. Favour was on Bundy's side, as he was not arrested and was eventually accepted into the Royal Canadian Air Force. After earning his wings and heading overseas, he was told that none of the white officers were willing to fly with him. A volunteer eventually stepped up and flew with the Black man. Bundy carried out several successful missions for his country and returned home alive, as a proud air force pilot.

Calvin shared these stories with a purpose and a point. He wanted to highlight the past while applauding the present and the positive changes that have been made with regards to one of Canada's minorities. After sharing these stories with his peers, he received letters from senators, thanking him for his speech and for educating others on the issue.

Heath Macquarrie, a former Member of Parliament and retired senator from Prince Edward Island, took the time to applaud Calvin for the words he shared on March 10, 1999, concerning enlistment into the Royal Canadian Navy: "The major theme of your fine speech is pertinent and shocking. These things have been too long with us. I liked your speech and hope you will make many more."

The letter touched Calvin, as it assured him that his words were not falling on deaf ears. He shared this with the former senator in a reply letter. "I was pleased to receive your comments on my speech on enlistment into the Royal Canadian Navy. I am still a rookie in the Senate and cannot gauge the impact of my words. Your letter is appreciated and encouraging." Calvin had now found his place in the Senate, and he was using it to represent the many faces he had seen and promised to help over the years.

After two years, Calvin's term in the Senate came to an end in 2000, when he reached the mandatory retirement age. He had accomplished what he had set out to do and then some. On June 19, as Doug and Joyce looked down from the gallery, in the same place they sat when Calvin was sworn in, Senator Ruck was honoured by his colleagues and new friends.

Nova Scotia Senator Alasdair B. Graham's speech expressed what everyone present felt: "Honourable senators, I think all of us in this chamber tonight have reflected at some time or another on the beautiful words of Dr. Martin Luther King, which he delivered in Memphis the day before his tragic death. He spoke about a dream, a dream that his children would one day live in a nation where they would not be judged by the colour of their skin but by the content of their character. That dream lived on. It lived on in all those people whose lives were shaped and guided by it and in all those people who believed that the challenges and injustices and inequities in life could always be beaten. Yes, they could always be beaten by the indomitable power of the human heart and the human spirit.

"Senator Calvin Woodrow Ruck has spent a long, fulfilling lifetime guided by that dream, guided by the content of his character. In all the years he worked as a labourer and a porter with the CNR, and as a cleaner at CFB Shearwater, he kept his heart and his mind focused squarely on the promised land of freedom. Whether he served in community development or as a social worker or as a human rights officer who played a key role in the desegregation of public accommodation, Cal always looked with the heart. He would give freely of his time and his energy to the Nova Scotia Association for the Advancement of Coloured Peoples [sic], among many others, winning a long list of honours in this country as a result.

"Tonight I refer to only a few of these, such as the Certificate of Honour from the Black Hall of Fame, the National Harry Jerome Award, along with an Honourary Doctor of Laws Degree from Dalhousie University. In 1995, he was made a member of the Order of Canada.

"Senator Ruck has spent a lifetime fighting for a country in which our children and our grandchildren will have the fair opportunity to do their very best, a country where they will have the right to grow up equal, a country where children would not be judged by the colour of their skin but by the content of their character.

"Calvin Ruck rarely missed an opportunity to proudly remind us in this chamber of the enormous contribution made to this country by Black veterans in both world wars. Tonight, we bid adieu to a man who has always distinguished himself from those who may have the privilege of sight but who do not have the rare gift of vision. He has distinguished himself from those who fail to understand that the real things in life, such as hope and compassion, tolerance and human rights, are often invisible to the eye.

"Calvin, it has been an honour and a privilege to have served with you in this chamber, and I join all honourable senators in wishing you and Joyce and Douglas – who is with his mother up in the gallery tonight – good health and much happiness in the years that lie ahead."

Calvin also had the chance to speak one more time to his fellow senators.

"Honourable senators, as my term in Ottawa draws to a close, I wish to express my thanks to all of those who have helped me along the way. I came here knowing very little, if anything, about the operations on Parliament Hill. My time spent here has been a wonderful experience. My wife has been with me all the way. She has been my right hand and she has done a very good job.

"I have learned a great deal about the federal government in Ottawa. As a boy growing up in Sydney, Nova Scotia, I was always aware of the Liberal presence. Many Cape Bretoners, for whatever reason, were Liberals. However, when people asked me what party I supported, I could not say because I had little experience in politics.

"My experience here has been very good. I have met some wonderful people who helped me along the way. I trust and pray that the Liberal Party will continue to be a light shining here in Ottawa. The party has made a difference, and I am sure it will continue to do so in the best interest of all Canadians."

In the summer of 2012 in Pictou, Nova Scotia, people gathered for the annual commemoration of the No. 2 Black Construction Battalion. As Doug and Jacqueline looked on, MP Peter Stoffer addressed the crowd and expressed his belief that Senator Ruck was one of the best senators in parliamentary history.

"I could see Doug was emotional about it," says Henry Bishop. "What Senator Ruck was able to do was bridge the gap across all the parliamentary lines. He wasn't NDP, he wasn't PC, he wasn't Liberal, Independent, Green Party; he was the one guy joining all forces. This is what he did; like me or don't like me. So he was the kind of man that strengthened the senators in their domain. Everything he did, he did for the bigger purpose. It wasn't for the recognition or limelight. He led by example."

Calvin's time in Ottawa was complete, at least for now. So with Joyce by his side, Senator Ruck flew back home to 27 Walker Street.

11: Leaving a Legacy

During Calvin's time in Ottawa, his family noticed he was becoming more forgetful. In his final year in the Senate, Calvin was diagnosed with Alzheimer's disease. Eventually, he was unable to work on his second book as he couldn't retain and process information in the same way.

"When first appointed to the Senate, he was still doing work on it, but two or three years later, he could not carry on with the project because his mind wasn't able to hold onto the thoughts. He may have been doing things but making no progress on it," says Doug. "He couldn't take it to the next step."

Suddenly Calvin was forgetting certain things he had worked so hard to achieve while in the Senate. "I took him over to the Camp Hill gravesite where members of the Black Battalion had been buried and they had put in special markers for them," explains Doug. "For whatever reason, this is where Dad's mind got stuck, so he would forget they had done it and want to go over and see if it had been done. On one occasion he and Mom took the ferry over to the graveyard to see these things and he asked me a few times to take him over, so the signs were starting to get there but we didn't know what was actually happening. We didn't know the Alzheimer's was trying to creep in."

Back in Nova Scotia, Doug spent more time at his parents' home, helping his father with different tasks. In 2000, Doug received news that he had been appointed vice-chair of the Canadian Industrial Relations Board in Ottawa. Without a second thought, Doug knew his mother and father would join his family in Ottawa. A family that had been through so much together was going to make the move together too.

"We were friends right to the end," says Wayne Adams. "When he moved to Ottawa that was like the end of an era. It was a good chapter in life. But we stayed in touch with letters. He was a real friend."

Calvin's life in Ottawa this time around was much different from the first. He enjoyed quiet days with Joyce and his family and stuck to a pretty straightforward routine. As his memory continued to deteriorate, he needed more assistance carrying out day-to-day tasks.

"It was awful," admits Jacqueline. "It was heartbreaking. It was strenuous. It was emotional. It was one of the worst experiences I think I've ever gone through. To witness someone who still probably could have done so much to help so many people and to have his mind be taken away from him – that was his greatest weapon. So once you took that away from him you disarmed him, so it was very difficult to see that happen."

To see a loved one vulnerable and helpless is one of the most painful sights. And yet he never completely lost himself. He still had strong opinions on world affairs and how his day should be run. His work ethic never ceased and he was still quite structured from sun-up to sundown. "No rest for the weary," he would say. He believed in his life having a purpose and he made certain that it always did until he was confined to bed. His passion for the past remained strong, as did his interest in the lives of his loved ones. His mind may have been fading, but his heart was just as big. It was his fight and wit and drive that got his family through the tough times of his final years. It was his encouragement, kind words and positive mentality that lifted spirits and reminded everyone that he's still Calvin and still has a lot to give.

"He would forget that his brother Winston had already passed," recalls Jacqueline. "He would forget that Martin Luther King, Jr. had passed, which is obviously not the Granddad I knew. He stayed the same in that he never once forgot to say grace before a meal. He was still happy, he was still gracious and he was still fun to be around."

A telling sign that he was still the man he had always been was evident when he attended a day program for those with Alzheimer's. "I would go to get him to drive him home and he would say, 'That was a good meeting we had today,'" recalls Doug with a smile. "One time we were walking out and there's these little older white ladies standing by and Dad goes to one and shakes her hand and says, 'That was a good meeting. It's good to see our people occupy these positions, sister.' And I was thinking, 'That poor woman has no idea what you're talking about, Dad.' She just said, 'Yes, that's true.' But that was his mind. Even at that stage he was thinking, 'How can we move things ahead?'"

Calvin spent his days doing what he had done every day of his life: working. He would wake up early and head down to the basement. With sounds of gospel music being wired from an upstairs stereo that Joyce controlled, Calvin would pick up his hammer and nails and begin to bang away at scraps of wood and beaten-up two-by-fours. He made dozens of these wooden flower boxes and enjoyed every minute of it. If there was a song he really enjoyed, he would put the hammer down, for thirty seconds at the most, and tap his cane to the beat.

Calvin was focused while he worked, but he did take breaks to talk to Valerie about life as a labourer. "He would say that he and I are the only people that do any work in this house because we were the only ones in the basement," Valerie recalls with a laugh. Calling Joyce the "bossy woman" and Doug the "tall guy," Calvin would share his thoughts and emphasize that the work is never done.

His only other breaks would be when Joyce called him up for lunch and dinner. The only other way of coaxing him upstairs to take a well-deserved rest was to mention a movie or documentary that he had most likely seen more than twenty times. Calvin would listen intently to a narrator speak of the heroics of the Tuskegee Airmen; he would shake his head in sadness and anger while listening to the accounts of the assassination of Martin Luther King, Jr. These memories were the freshest in his mind. "He had this amazing memory of the past and yet he couldn't remember where he put his glasses," laughs Henry Bishop.

Calvin also never forgot his faith, as Doug recounts. "If you ever wanted to see someone who could give you a confidence in faith, it was Dad. Even in his later days. His mind has been addled by Alzheimer's and he's in bed singing hymns and giving praise to God. It was the most extraordinary thing to see. And you would say, there's something here. People who get Alzheimer's can become irate and angry because those social constraints are gone, but this was the same man. The same pleasant man."

On the morning of October 19, 2004, at the age of seventy-nine, Calvin died in his home in Ottawa. "It was one of those very tragic things that his life, though long in its way, was short in many ways," says Bridglal Pachai.

Upon the announcement of Calvin's death, the Senate of Canada and House of Commons paid tribute to their colleague. The stories Calvin had been telling for so many years were now being told by others – a true testament to the great legacy that is Calvin's life.

Jack Austin, Leader of the Government in the Senate, told members he had done some research to learn more about Senator Ruck. He said, "What I have found is so beautifully expressed in *The Daily News*, which is a Halifax newspaper, in an editorial that they issued on October 22 last. I should like to read portions of the editorial into the record. It states:

"They are called "The Greatest Generation." Born between the years 1910 and 1930, its surviving members are senior citizens now – grandparents and great-grandparents. Some continue to live in proud independence; others reside in nursing homes. They are enduring the infirmities of age with the same stoic spirit that carried them through the privations of the Great Depression and the horrors of the Second World War, the events that shaped their lives.

"We are losing them: one by one, day by day.

"Calvin Ruck was a member of the Greatest Generation. He passed away at the age of 79 on Tuesday in Ottawa, where he had lived during the past several years. It was the end of a journey that took him from Whitney Pier in Sydney to Parliament Hill in Ottawa; from a job as a sleeping-car porter on the Canadian National Railway to a seat in Canada's Senate.

"Between those poles of his life, Mr. Ruck could best be described as a one-man civil-rights movement. As a Black man, the son of immigrants from Barbados, he faced not only the tough and trying times of the 1930s and '40s, when the world was shaken to its roots, and then reshaped; he also bore the brunt of racism at a time when it was not only fashionable, but acceptable.

"He did more than just bear it, though. He fought it in a diligent and dignified manner. No challenge was too great for him to accept, and overcome.

"The Nova Scotia Association for the Advancement of Coloured People? He was on its executive.

"The Nova Scotia Human Rights Commission? He was a rights officer and a commissioner.

"The Stevens Road United Baptist Church? He was a deacon.

"The Black Cultural Society of Nova Scotia? He was its treasurer.

"A complete list of the organizations to which Mr. Ruck contributed, and the awards he won would fill the rest of this space.

"Aside from his tenure in the Senate, which ran from 1998 to 2000, Mr. Ruck is best remembered for single-handedly rescuing an important piece of Canadian military history from an obscurity it did not deserve. Outlandish as it seems now, during the First World War, a debate raged over whether Blacks were worthy to serve in the Canadian military. The government formed an all-Black unit called the No. 2 Construction Battalion, which served overseas during the conflict. Although it attracted recruits from other parts of Canada and the United States, most of its members were Nova Scotians.

"After the war ended, the unit was largely forgotten.

"But not by Mr. Ruck. After years of diligent research, he published a book called *The Black Battalion: 1916-1920: Canada's Best Kept Military Secret*, which accorded the soldiers the recognition they deserved.

"Mr. Ruck's many accomplishments were no secret. His life set an example for people of all generations – and all colours."

Calling Calvin "a great Canadian and a great Nova Scotian," then Senator Donald H. Oliver spoke of the funeral service: "Saturday's funeral was a fitting tribute. Hundreds of people filled the Atlantic Funeral Home in Dartmouth to its capacity. Several prominent religious figures gave fitting inspirational tributes. The gospel music that filled the building throughout the afternoon brought tears to our eyes, and I know it would have made the senator proud.

"Calvin's two sons, Martin and Douglas Ruck, gave a heartfelt eulogy of their father's work to promote the rights of Blacks in Canada. Martin told the story of how Calvin Ruck broke down the barrier to let Black people have their hair cut in white barbershops by staging a number of barbershop sit-ins. This was just one example of how he methodically broke down systemic barriers and promoted racial equality in Canada."

Senator Oliver went on to quote from Calvin's obituary: "'Calvin Ruck was not a man who wished for change but, rather, one who worked to make a difference. His efforts in Nova Scotia have reverberated throughout the nation. He believed in a society that treated all people, regardless of their colour, with respect and dignity.'

"Honourable senators, Calvin Ruck was a tireless advocate for racial equality, a dedicated supporter of equal rights and a great Canadian. He will be missed."

Another Nova Scotia senator, Wilfred P. Moore, recounted "two anecdotes ... [that] are testaments to the soulful motivation and high quality of Senator Ruck's work.

"As mentioned by Senator Austin, Senator Ruck wrote two books about the history of Canada's Black Battalion, No. 2 Construction, which he called 'Canada's best-kept military secret.' One Wednesday at National Liberal Caucus – I ask that partisans indulge me this one little indiscretion – Senator Ruck took the microphone and through the chair he asked Prime Minister Chrétien to cause markers to be placed at the unmarked graves of Black veterans who served Canada. In his respectful way, he assured the Prime Minister that he did possess the power to address this situation and that it was the right and respectful thing to do. That Gandhi-like approach by Senator Ruck moved our Prime Minister to direct the minister responsible to confer immediately with the good senator in an anteroom and to fulfil his request. Those markers were put in place forthwith, thanks to that intervention by Senator Ruck.

"Senator Ruck was a devout Christian. At his going home celebration his son, Douglas, shared the following story with the host of family and friends gathered. Two uniformed police officers, one Black and one white, came to Douglas' residence in the company of the funeral home staff to receive the senator's remains. As he was laid to rest in the vehicle, both officers stood alongside, came to attention and snapped a salute. That gesture was a moment of discrimination-free respect, the paramount thing that motivated Senator Ruck in all of his work.

"Sometimes, honourable senators, we do not realize the giant qualities of the men and women with whom we associate on a day-to-day basis.

"We extend our deepest sympathy to the late Senator Ruck's spouse, Joyce, their sons, Douglas and Martin, and his brother, Arthur, and we thank them for sharing this outstanding man with us."

In the House of Commons, Michael John Savage, then the Member of Parliament for Dartmouth, stood to honour a man who had worked side by side with his father for so many years. "Mr. Speaker, I rise today to honour a great Canadian, a true civil rights hero in Nova Scotia, who passed away last week. His son Martin told me last week that the most amazing thing about his father was his humility. This was a remarkably humble man who made the world better in so many ways."

Calvin had left a legacy. His life was being remembered and honoured on a national level and it was all because he decided one day to stand up, be heard and lead by example. "He was early among people who did social development-type work of any type," says Joan Gilroy, who speaks of Calvin as a pioneer. "That was kind of a new field. And he did it primarily in Black communities. He was in a new section of our field of social work but also applying it in a different area, a different race, and providing services that would be useful to the community. He worked with people who lived in different communities on what it is that they saw that they needed for their community. It could be a school or a daycare or sports, different things like that. He was very involved with the people. Trying to work with the people on the issues that they felt were important, that would build their communities.

"I think like all pioneers, he just didn't give up. He just persisted. He was very determined, but he had a lovely, lovely way of being determined and persisting. You couldn't fault him or get angry with him. You were just trying to figure out what more can we do here. You're working for goals that are community goals, not just your personal goals. It was a very difficult time where there was physical danger involved in standing up for what was right. For anyone, really, and certainly for Black people in Canada at that time. That was really scary."

During Black History Month, Valerie, an elementary school teacher, ensures that all of her students know Calvin Ruck. "Everybody past grade two knows Calvin Ruck. They love it. I start with Martin Luther King, Jr. in January and then say Calvin was the Martin Luther King of Nova Scotia."

In 2005, Calvin became the first recipient of Ottawa's Dream Keeper Award, an honour created to remember the life and work of Martin Luther King, Jr. One year after his death, Calvin's family would accept this posthumous award on his behalf.

"Every step of the way it has been admiration," says Carolyn Thomas, "and even in death, I look at him as the giant that he was – *and is* – in my life. He personified dignity and a real interest in people. Even though he was done by, he didn't carry that against people. And I think people saw that in him, the human aspect of him. He was just a caring man. The legacy is great."

"Of all the things that he was really admired for, he was pure as the driven snow in terms of his integrity and I felt that above all," says Henry Bishop. "He always said to me, you know people are not going to trust you just because of your name; you have to earn your reputation and become good-natured and good-spirited. He said your integrity can be snatched away from you like that. It doesn't matter how smart you are, how much money you have, what neighbourhood you live in, your integrity is something that will live with you forever and your legacy will continue on. You can feel that in the Ruck family. He went into some fiery pits but came out pretty much unscathed and came out a better man for it."

While there were the great memories of his outstanding accomplishments, his loved ones also had the personal, simple memories – those are the ones that would be remembered and missed the most.

"We would play this game where one person would hum a song and the others would have to guess what it is and we played this on a Sunday afternoon after Nanny made us lunch," explains Jacqueline. "I miss hearing him sing. He would hum very quietly so we could barely hear him, which we all found funny. And he always got excited when we would guess it, although often times he would be singing obscure songs we never heard of. It was either an obscure song or the 'Battle Hymn of the Republic.'

"I miss hearing him ask me about school. He would call me Jackliner. He would say, 'How's school going, Jackliner?' I miss just walking into Nanny's house and seeing him smile and hug me. I also miss going to church with him because he really got a lot out of church. If there was a song that he knew, he sang it with all his might. There was a conviction behind the words he was singing because he believed those words. I miss things like that."

Both Ottawa and Halifax newspapers printed tribute pieces following the announcement of Calvin's death. A local hero had passed away and entire communities wanted to show their respect.

"In all of my travels, I've never heard anybody say anything bad about Dr. Ruck," says Henry Bishop. "He was a great example for anybody who wanted to make a difference in this world. That's the epitome of greatness. Of feeling that you have a purpose, that you have to make people feel that they have a purpose and that's what he did for me. He was a good example of it doesn't matter where you start; it's where you end up. It doesn't matter where you come from; it's what you do with your life."

Calvin was buried in Dartmouth, Nova Scotia, and his funeral, held at the Atlantic Funeral Home on Main Street in Dartmouth, was a celebration of life. Those who were once his adversaries showed up to pay their final respects.

"Even people who lived on Walker Street that were still living were at the funeral," says Joyce. As the main chapel became standing room only, a separate room within the building was designated for overflow, with televisions streaming the celebration of Calvin's life. Family members and loved ones sang his favourite songs, recited his favourite Bible verses and told stories that made those present smile but also reflect on what an amazing man he truly was.

"When we die, we take none of our material gifts or goods with us," says Jacqueline, "and people won't remember us by what we had or how we looked, but they'll remember us by what we've done and what kind of person we were and I think that when we lost Granddad, his legacy just continued on. The things he did will last forever."

During the eulogy, Doug recounted the day his father had passed away and, just as Wilfred Moore had mentioned, Doug spoke of the welcome coincidence of the two policemen who came to the door that day.

He was placed into a hearse, wrapped in a Canadian flag and saluted by the officers. It was fitting that one Black man and one white man gave Calvin his final salute, as it signified what he had worked so hard to achieve his whole life – equality.

The winds of change have blown indeed.

Conclusion

Writing this book allowed me to reflect on my own fond memories of my grandfather. While it was incredible to see him receive an honourary doctorate, watch as he humbly spoke at an event created solely to celebrate his success, and look on as he was sworn into the Senate of Canada, my fondest memories are the more intimate times: the Friday night and Sunday afternoon dinners on Walker Street where he would show me his garden and take pictures of my sister and me running around the lawn; the rides in the car where he would ask me my multiplication tables and test my spelling abilities; and sitting next to him at church and seeing the smile cross his face as he would sing at the top of his lungs when an old hymn began. These are the things that make me smile because they are the memories when it was just me and Granddad. I cherish those times most.

While those memories are simple, the impact my grandfather had on my life is immense. I most admire his tenacity and drive, and strive to model those characteristics in my daily life. Nothing was ever handed to him. He moved up societal ranks through hard work and was constantly forced to prove himself in the face of adversity. This taught me that everyone, no matter upbringing or social status, has a choice in life. My grandfather chose to always create a better day than the day before.

Nelson Mandela once said, "I have walked that long road to freedom. I have tried not to falter; I have made missteps along the way. But I have discovered the secret that after climbing a great hill, one only finds that there are many more hills to climb. I have taken a moment here to rest, to steal a view of the glorious vista that surrounds me, to look back on the distance I have come. But I can only rest for a moment, for with freedom come responsibilities, and I dare not linger, for my long walk is not ended."

My grandfather's work was never done. There was always room for improvement and there was no such thing as a missed opportunity. From the time he was a young boy, he dreamt of a better life, but unlike dreamers, he brought that life into existence.

Leaving a great legacy allows future generations to look back at the success story of one's life. But the impact of that legacy is only immortal if we choose to not only reflect, but, more importantly, advance. My grandfather taught me that we cannot just sit on the sidelines waiting for change to happen. Everyone, no matter race or social status, has a responsibility to advocate for civil rights and equality. The legwork has already been done and the stage has already been set. Future generations just have to take the torch and run with it, for there will always be another great hill to climb.

After all, as my grandfather taught me, the sky's the limit.

DISCARD